History of
the Mass

History of the Mass

Robert Cabié

Translated by
Lawrence J. Johnson

PASTORAL PRESS
PORTLAND · OREGON

Translated from the French
Histoire de la Messe
Desclée, Paris
1990

ISBN 0-912405-97-X

© 1992 Pastoral Press
A Division of OCP Publications
5536 N.E. Hassalo
Portland OR 97213
Phone 800-LITURGY (548-8749)
Email: liturgy@ocp.org
Web site: www.pastoralpress.com
Web site: www.ocp.org

Contents

Foreword

Without doubt, the decisions of Vatican II that most affect people are those belonging to the liturgy, especially the Mass. At Mass changes determined by the Council are visible to regular worshipers each Sunday and to others who celebrate the Mass only at weddings and funerals or on Easter and Christmas. These liturgical changes are perceived as having upset, even overthrown, established practice, as having distanced us from the world in which everything was familiar. Whether one is happy or unhappy in the church, images treasured since childhood are the measure of "all that is new." But how long had the Mass existed unchanged in the form that it had before the Council's reforms?

Some Christians speak about "the Mass of Pius V" as though it had no precedents, yet Pius V lived only four hundred years ago; how was the Mass celebrated before him? As soon as we exceed the boundaries of two or three generations, memory reassures us: the forms of celebration that we have just abandoned are the Mass "as it was always done." Other Christians, with perhaps a larger grasp of history, are happy that the decisions of Vatican II have brought about a return to the sources. They know that St. Gregory the Great, for example, celebrated Mass facing the people, and that the East has always had other forms of celebrating this sacrament. Can we not, therefore, allow for an organic development of the rites of the Mass since the apostolic period?

Finally, still other Christians, the younger generation, know the Mass only as it is celebrated today. The young hear grand allusions to the past — to a ritual pattern that seemed to express more fully, even to guarantee, the dignity, majesty, and security of the "true Catholic faith." But they have also been told that the changes of Vatican II restored to Christians a form of prayer that many fervent Catholics had long desired.

1

Do not these reflections demonstrate the benefits to be gained from a patient historical inquiry into the Mass as a human institution, which—like all things human, even the human encounter with God—has known both glory and vicissitude throughout the centuries? The Mass, having its origin in the will of the Lord, has never been other than what it was in the beginning, and yet, throughout history, the Mass has been experienced by people of various races, languages, and civilizations, people who brought to the celebration their own piety and culture—and perhaps also their weaknesses. Without damaging its fundamental structure, people have given the Mass, according to different times and places, different visible forms. We must understand, as the Christians before us did, that fidelity does not necessarily consist in reproducing models inherited from one's forebears but in penetrating the mystery we have received and in bringing to it all the richness of one's own age and culture, before we, too, pass this mystery on to our children.

Together, therefore, we are about to set off on a pilgrimage. Our guides will be those who have studied the ancient books and those who have given witness (now and throughout the ages) that their spiritual experience was nourished by the sacrament of the altar. We can only take the main roads without pausing, as pleasant as that would be, at each turn along the way.

We will study this history as it unfolded, successively, in five major periods:

• the Mass before the formation of liturgical books, from the New Testament to the end of the third century (chapter 1);

• the creative period in which various structural elements of the celebration were expanded. Here we will separate earlier embellishments brought forth in the various churches during the fourth and fifth centuries (chapters 2 and 3) from the elaborate forms that appeared during the sixth to the eighth centuries (chapter 4);

• the changes that appeared during the Carolingian period concerning the priest's role in the Mass (chapter 5); and the changes that began in the twelfth century that had so large an effect on eucharistic piety (chapter 6);

• the Mass as it appeared in the missal published by Pius V after the Council of Trent (chapter 7); and the popular devotions and piety that accompanied the implementation of this missal (chapter 8); and

• finally, the liturgical movement that began in the nineteenth century and culminated in the Second Vatican Council (chapter 9); and the Mass as it was reformed in the missal of Paul VI in 1970 (chapter 10).

Our focus throughout this journey, but especially from Chapter 4 on, will be on the Roman tradition, since it is from this tradition that our present practice is derived. The road we will follow is historical; it will lead us to a better understanding of the content and manner of the church's prayer, that is, what the church has done and is still doing when it celebrates the eucharist.

General Bibliography

Robert Cabié. *The Eucharist.* Vol. 2 of *The Church at Prayer.* Edited by Aimé Georges Martimort. Translated by Matthew J. O'Connell. Collegeville: The Liturgical Press, 1986.

Johannes H. Emminghaus. *The Eucharist: Essence, Form, Manifestation.* Translated by Matthew J. O'Connell. Collegeville: The Liturgical Press, 1978.

Edward Foley. *From Age to Age: How Christians Celebrated the Eucharist.* Chicago: Liturgy Training Publications, 1991.

Joseph A. Jungmann. *The Mass of the Roman Rite: Its Origins and Development.* 2 Vols. Translated by Francis A. Brunner. New York: Benziger Brothers, 1951, 1955.

Joseph A. Jungmann. *The Mass of the Roman Rite: Its Origins and Development.* Vol. 1 of *Missarum Sollemnia.* Translated by Francis A. Brunner. Revised by Charles K. Riepe. New York: Benziger Brothers, 1959.

Theodor Klauser. *A Short History of the Western Liturgy: An Account and Some Reflections.* Translated by John Halliburton. York: Oxford University Press, 1969.

Herman Wegman. *Christian Worship in East and West: A Study Guide to Liturgical History.* Translated by Gordon W. Lathrop. New York: Pueblo Publishing Company, 1985.

Chapter I

From the Last Supper to the Mass
I - III century

"Do this in memory of me"

At his last meal before being handed over to Roman authorities, before undergoing his passion and being raised from the dead, Jesus memorializes his death and resurrection; that is, he creates the ritual form of his passover to the Father so that his disciples and later generations of Christians may participate in and relive those events until he comes again at the end of time.

Did Jesus celebrate the Jewish Passover at the Last Supper? The record is unclear, but in any case, the Gospels present Jesus as inaugurating the new Passover. He is the lamb of God whose blood is poured out "for you and for many," the new and definitive covenant, our paschal mystery.

The history of the Mass begins with the command of the Lord as recounted by Paul and Luke (1 Cor 11:24; Lk 22:19): "Do this in memory of me," namely, do what Jesus himself did when eating with his disciples before his death on the cross. But the New Testament offers no description, in our sense of the term, of what Jesus actually did or said at that meal. Accounts describing the institution of the eucharist were written years after the event—Paul's account being the earliest (ca. 55)—and even then, their purpose was not to recreate history but to allow Christians of every generation to deepen their understanding of a habit that had become second nature to them—the churches' habit of gathering together to "break bread."

The First Letter to the Corinthians shows this very clearly: when the Christians at Corinth began having difficulties in carrying out a rite that was already deeply rooted in the life of their community, Paul decides to recall the rite's true meaning by referring it back to its life-setting in the Last Supper. The Supper, therefore, and the Lord's command that recalls it, are not so much history as the very ground and reason for the Corinthians' present actions.

Paul uses the Lord's command to reprove abuses and to discover again "the tradition that comes from the Lord." He approached the Last Supper as a foundational event—as the touchstone of the Corinthians' present way of life. And the same is true for the institution accounts in the first three Gospels. (John's presentation of the Last Supper has a different context and does not concern us here.) Even if these scriptural accounts, drawing on the actions and words repeated at each celebration, are based on somewhat edited or organized notes, their purpose is to recount the spiritual experiences of the various churches in which the Gospels were written. Thus, the "narratives" of the Last Supper are neither historical documents nor news reports; they are more akin to a narrative explanation, or catechesis, on the sacrament of Christ's body and blood. Well before these accounts were elaborated, the eucharist had become part of the life of the Christian community.

Nevertheless, our curiosity is aroused. How can we not seek to discover what happened in the midst of this most memorable meal? We look, therefore, at the tradition of table prayer that was familiar to Jesus and his disciples and well-established in the Judaism of his time. When it was Jesus' time to preside at table, he would have said the customary prayers—called "blessings"—and he would certainly have used his legitimate freedom of introducing adaptations, perhaps to the extent of giving new meaning to old words. As a matter of fact, in oral tradition formularies were handed down as schematic patterns, patterns based on certain expressions that were known by heart, and it was on the basis of these patterns that a certain freedom in composition was allowed.

One possible structure of these ritual meals we know from Luke's Gospel: first the wine is prepared, then the host and guests drink, each in turn. A formula is attached to this action: "Blessed art thou, Lord our God, king of the universe, who gives us the fruit of the vine." Is it not significant that the words "fruit of the vine" are found on the lips of Jesus, who was the first to take the cup?

The table liturgy itself began when the father of the family took the bread that he was going to distribute to the guests: "Blessed art thou, Lord . . . who brings forth bread from the earth." And when the meal ended, he said a longer formula, the "great blessing," over the cup that had been refilled. The Lord is blessed for food and for the "earth," and praise is transformed

6

The Last Supper

The First Letter of St. Paul to the Corinthians (11:20-26)

When you meet in one place, then, is it not to eat the Lord's supper, for in eating, each one goes ahead with his own supper, and one goes hungry while another gets drunk. Do you not have houses in which you can eat and drink? Or do you show contempt for the church of God and make those who have nothing feel ashamed? What can I say to you? Shall I praise you? In this manner I do not praise you. For I received from the Lord what I also handed on to you, that the Lord Jesus, on the night he was handed over . . .

The Gospel according to St. Luke (22:14-20)

When the hour came, he took his place at table with the apostles. He said to them, "I have eagerly desired to eat this Passover with you before I suffer, for, I tell you, I shall not eat it [again] until there is fulfillment in the kingdom of God."

He then took a cup, gave thanks, and said, "Take this and share it among yourselves, for I tell you [that] from this time on I shall not drink of the fruit of the vine until the kingdom of God comes."

Then he took the bread, said the blessing, broke it, and gave it to them, saying, "This is my body which will be given for you; do this in memory of me."

And likewise the cup after they had eaten, saying, "This cup is the new covenant in my blood, which will be shed for you."

The Gospel according to St. Mark (14:22-25)

While they were eating, he took bread, said the blessing, broke it, and gave it to them, and said, "Take it, this is my body." He then took a cup, gave thanks, and gave it to them, and they all drank from it. He said to them, "This is my blood of the covenant which shall be shed for many. Amen, I say to you, I shall not drink again the fruit of the vine until the day when I drink it in the new kingdom of God.

into supplication so that the wonders of God may still be accomplished today. Here we find one of the distinctive features of biblical prayer. A style of addressing the Father, a "spirituality," is expressed by means of a twofold literary form: first, we contemplate God and God's great deeds in the past; second, we joyfully recognize God's gifts to us (to the speaker) and request that similar blessings may appear in our time.

Surely the Lord's words concerning his body are to be situated at the beginning of the meal, while those concerning his blood were said "after the meal": quite probably this pattern accounts for Paul's use of only these moments.

The Gospels of Matthew and Mark—few differences exist between them—refer to a more elaborate tradition, as if the most ancient witnesses had been reworked. These evangelists do not speak of the first cup, but attach Christ's words to the cup of wine at the end of the meal. Yet they especially situate the actions concerning the bread and wine "during the meal," without giving further details, as though these actions immediately followed one another. This version is probably explained by liturgical practices. Very early, the eucharist had ceased to be celebrated within the framework of the Jewish table ritual, even if the participants ate a meal before or after the eucharist. As a result, the authors of the first two Gospels could omit details that no longer corresponded to the experience of their communities.

We have, therefore, two traditional accounts of the institution of the eucharist (Paul and Luke's and Matthew and Mark's). In each of these two accounts the structure is the same, and can easily be recapped in a succession of four verbs. The fourth verb, it is true, is not found in Paul, but can be easily supplied by the context. The structure is this:

1. Jesus *takes* bread and a cup of wine;
2. He *gives thanks*, or says a blessing;
3. He *breaks* the bread; and
4. He *gives* [it] as food to his disciples.

This structure has determined the pattern for the second part of the Mass:

1. The preparation of the gifts: the assembly offers bread and wine;
2. the eucharistic prayer (including the institution account);
3. the breaking of the bread; and
4. the communion.

"He explained to them, the Scriptures . . ."

The presence of these four verbs in other New Testament passages indicates that these other passages also refer to the Last Supper or at least

The Disciples on the Road to Emmaus

Now that very day two of them were going to a village seven miles from Jerusalem called Emmaus, and they were conversing about all the things that had occurred.

And it happened that while they were conversing and debating, Jesus himself drew near and walked with them, but their eyes were prevented from recognizing him. He asked them, "What are you discussing as you walk along?" They stopped, looking downcast. One of them, named Cleopas, said to him in reply, "Are you the only visitor to Jerusalem who does not know of the things that have taken place there in these days?" . . .

And he said to them, "Oh, how foolish you are! How slow of heart to believe all that the prophets spoke! Was it not necessary that the Messiah should suffer these things and enter into his glory? Then beginning with Moses and all the prophets, he interpreted to them what referred to him in all the scriptures . . .

And it happened that when he was with them at table, he took bread, said the blessing, broke it, and gave it to them. With that their eyes were opened and they recognized him, but he disappeared from their sight. Then they said to each other, "Were not our hearts burning [within us] while he spoke to us on the way and opened the scriptures to us?"

Luke 24:13-32

A Sunday at Troas

On the first day of the week when we gathered to break bread, Paul spoke to them because he was going to leave on the next day, and he kept on speaking till midnight . . . then he returned upstairs, broke the bread, and ate.

Acts of the Apostles 20:7-11

Letter from the Governor of Bithynia
to the Emperor of Rome

It is my custom, sir, to refer to you in all cases where I do not feel sure . . . I have never been present at any legal examination of the Christians, and I do not know, therefore, what are the usual penalties passed upon them, or the limits of these penalties . . .

Some, whose names were given me by an informer, first said that they had been Christian but were no longer, some of them having recanted many years before, and more than one so long as twenty years back. They all worshiped your image and the statues of the deities, and cursed the name of Christ.

But they declared that the sum of their guilt or their error only amounted to this, that on a stated day they had been accustomed to meet before daybreak and to recite a hymn among themselves to Christ, as though he were a god, and that so far from binding themselves by oath to commit any crime, their oath was to abstain from theft, robbery, adultery, and from breach of faith, and not to deny trust-money placed in their keeping when called to deliver it. When this ceremony was concluded, it had been their custom to depart and meet again to take food; but it was of no special character and quite harmless, and they had ceased this practice after the edict in which, in accordance with your orders, I had forbidden all secret societies.

Pliny the Younger, Letter Written to Trajan in 112

evoke this meal. This connection is especially true of the accounts of the multiplication of the bread (see, for example, Mk 6:30-44) and the episode at Emmaus, which took place on the evening of the resurrection (Lk 24:13-32). At Emmaus, the disciples recognize the Lord in the breaking of the bread. Yet their recognition of him at table is based on their previous experience; they had, after all, walked and talked with him along the way: "Were not our hearts burning [within us] while he spoke to us on the way and opened the scriptures to us?" (v. 32).

This story is undoubtedly a community's meditation on the way it celebrates the eucharist. The community begins its gathering by reference to the holy books and by announcing that the promises made to Israel are now being fulfilled. At first this witness is a living voice, Paul's voice, for example, when the faithful at Troas gather around him to "break the bread." But a progressive evolution ensues: the witnesses write their memoirs, and these texts are received with the same esteem accorded the texts of the Old Testament. As the apostles disappear, the tradition that had its life-setting in their midst came to be celebrated according to a set pattern that was like the pattern followed in the Jewish synagogue. Even though most Christians no longer participated in the Jewish assemblies, this model of the liturgy came to be followed in their own gatherings.

Organizing the Rites of the Mass

The structure of the Mass, as it will be universally followed, is established as early as the second century. Indeed it is already complete in Justin's description of the Sunday assembly (ca. 150). Justin, though not a Jew, was a native of Palestine and a convert to the Gospel; later he established a school of philosophy at Rome to refute openly the calumnious rumors being told about Christ's disciples. His description of the Sunday assembly is in his Second Apology.

On this day of the Sun, Justin wrote, the faithful are called together, and there is but one celebration: people do not go all over but hasten to the same place. Their gathering is organized: its leader is a "presider." This term here designates the bishop whose function is not merely liturgical or cultic, since he also provides for the needs of the poor. Other ministers to the gathering are deacons and readers.

Once the people have assembled, the liturgy of the word takes place, with its readings, homily, and general prayer. There is reason to believe that the Scriptures were read in a continuous fashion, beginning each time at the place where the previous gathering had ended and continuing for "as long as time permits." These readings are the "memoirs of the apostles," namely, the New Testament. But the Old Testament is also read; for this

The Mass at Rome in the Middle
of the Second Century

And on the day called Sunday, all who live in cities or in the country gather together in one place, and the memoirs of the apostles or the writings of the prophets are read, as long as time permits; then, when the reader has ceased, the president verbally instructs, and exhorts to the imitation of these good things.

Then we all rise together and pray, and, as we before said, when our prayer is ended, bread and wine and water are brought, and the president in like manner offers prayers and thanksgivings according to his ability, and the people assent, saying Amen; and there is a distribution to each, and a participation of that over which thanks have been given, and to those who are absent a portion is sent by the deacons.

And they who are well to do, and willing, give what each thinks fit; and what is collected is deposited with the president, who succors the orphans and widows, and those who, through sickness or any other cause, are in want, and those who are in bonds, and the strangers sojourning among us, and in a word takes care of all those who are in need.

* * * * * *

And this food among us is called the eucharist, of which no one is allowed to partake but the man who believes that the things which we teach are true, and who has been washed with the washing that is for the remission of sins, and unto regeneration, and who is so living as Christ has enjoined. For not as common bread and common drink do we receive these; but in like manner as Jesus Christ our Savior, having been made flesh by the Word of God, had both flesh and blood for our salvation, so likewise we have been taught that the food which is blessed by the prayer of His word, and from which our blood and flesh by transmutation are nourished, is the flesh and blood of that Jesus who was made flesh.

St. Justin, First Apology
Addressed to Antonius Pius (138-161),
Chapters 66:3 and 67:3-6

collection is undoubtedly what Justin meant by the "writings of the prophets."

Following the readings, the presider exhorts everyone to put into practice these teachings of the Lord. Earlier, Justin had mentioned the eucharist in a chapter devoted to baptism and there referred to the "common prayers" said "for ourselves, for the neophytes [the newly baptized], and for people everywhere." In that same chapter he mentioned the kiss of peace. The presider's homily, the general intercessions and the kiss of peace are responses to the reading.

The liturgy of the eucharist begins as Jesus must have begun the Last Supper. To this point the table has been bare; now, with all looking on, "bread, wine, and water" are brought forward. The use of water should not surprise us: in ancient times people always diluted their wine. It was too strong to be taken unadulterated, unless, of course, one was drinking to become intoxicated.

Then come the "prayers and thanksgivings" (the Greek word for "thanksgiving" is *eucharistia*). This term is the consecratory formula; no longer are the bread and wine "ordinary food"; they have become "eucharistic" because the thanksgiving has been said. The word "eucharist" will even become the name for this food: "This food among us is called the eucharist." Notice how Justin stresses the participation of all who "assent" to this thanksgiving by acclaiming the "Amen."

The communion is surely preceded by the breaking of the bread, though the latter action is not mentioned. The distribution is very succinctly described: the deacons give the eucharist to the faithful who are present, and they also carry these gifts to those who are absent.

"And the presider in like manner offers prayers and thanksgivings according to his ability." What lies beneath Justin's expression in this instance? Can we picture how the early church passed from the Jewish blessing prayers that Jesus knew and probably used at the Last Supper to the Christian eucharistic prayer?

The Prayer of the *Didache*

The apostles, desiring to obey the Lord's command, must have imitated Jesus' behavior at the Supper, namely, by sharing a ritual meal and saying the same words. Perhaps a witness of this is found in the *Didache*, which repeats the three moments mentioned by Luke: "First for the cup . . . then for the bread broken . . . and when your hunger has been satisfied. . . ." The word "eucharist," which introduces this part of the text, does not correspond to just any prayer of thanksgiving, since we are also told that it is

The Prayer of the *Didache*

9. Regarding the Eucharist. Give thanks as follows:
First, concerning the cup:
We give Thee thanks, Our Father, for the Holy Vine of David Thy servant, which Thou hast made known to us through Jesus, Thy Servant.

To Thee be the glory for evermore.
Next, concerning the broken bread:
We give Thee thanks, Our Father, for the life and knowledge which Thou hast made known to us through Jesus, Thy Servant.

To Thee be the glory forevermore.
As this broken bread was scattered over the hills and then, when gathered, become one mass, so may Thy Church be gathered from the ends of the earth into Thy Kingdom. For Thine is the glory and the power through Jesus Christ forevermore.

Let no one eat and drink of your eucharist but those baptized in the name of the Lord . . .

10. After you have taken your fill of food, give thanks as follows:
We give Thee thanks, O Holy Father, for Thy holy name which Thou hast enshrined in our hearts, and for the knowledge and faith and immortality which Thou hast made known to us through Jesus, Thy Servant.

To Thee be the glory for evermore.
Thou, Lord Almighty, has created all things for the sake of Thy name and hast given food and drink for men to enjoy, that they may give thanks to Thee; but to us Thou hast vouchsafed spiritual food and drink and eternal life through Jesus, Thy Servant.

Above all, we give Thee thanks because Thou art mighty.
To Thee be the glory for evermore.
Remember, O Lord, Thy Church: deliver her from all evil, perfect her in Thy love, and from the four winds assemble her, the sanctified, in Thy kingdom which Thou hast prepared for her.

For Thine is the power and the glory for evermore.
May Grace come, and this world pass away!
Hosanna to the God of David!
If anyone is holy, let him advance; if anyone is not, let him be converted. Maranatha!
Amen.

14

food and drink, "let no one eat or drink of your eucharist except . . ." It is, moreover, food and drink that is reserved to the baptized.

Admittedly, however, the account of the institution does not appear in the *Didache*. Could it have been simply omitted? Certainly not, for it is "in memory" of Christ that the church follows his example. Further, the accounts of the institution in 1 Corinthians and the Gospels are based on a stereotype which, with its four key verbs, seems to have been memorized for use in the celebration. Perhaps the account was said at the outset of the gathering, as the flight from Egypt is remembered at the beginning of the Jewish Passover meal. Not until later years will this formula be introduced within the course of the prayer.

This explanation is only a hypothesis. It suggests, however, that the texts that lie behind the *Didache* are very ancient, as old or older than "the memoirs of the apostles." Perhaps they circulated as early as the years 50 to 70 and were only in the second century incorporated into this compilation called the *Didache*.

The Eucharistic Prayer in the Third Century

During the second century, the practice of celebrating the eucharist during the course of a meal with a plurality of blessings was abandoned. By the third century, only one prayer of praise and supplication remains, similar to the blessing that concludes the Jewish table liturgy.

But something new is also introduced: a combination of two elements is inserted within the heart of the composition. First, the "memory" or anamnesis expressing the immediacy of the eucharistic action: "we offer" the body and blood of Christ by "making memory" of his death and resurrection. Second, the institution account lays the foundation for this "memory" and supports this reenactment of the Last Supper, whose renewal has been entrusted to the church.

Some of the most ancient prayers combine these two elements; but most often they appear in succession and remain on a par with one another. The institution account soon assumes the dominant position. In fact, the church seems always to have a tendency to consider this account as a separate unit, thereby isolating the words of Christ, "This is my body . . . This is my blood," from the rest of the prayer.

The first text of a eucharistic prayer or anaphora that has come down to us goes back to the year 225; it is found in the *Apostolic Tradition* attributed to Hippolytus of Rome. The prayer is presented as a simple model for presbyters, because at this time oral tradition holds sway. It begins with an introductory dialogue inviting all to "give thanks" or to

A Eucharistic Prayer from the Third Century

—The Lord be with you!   — And with your spirit!

—Let us lift up our hearts.   — They are turned to the Lord!

—Let us give thanks to the Lord.   — It is right and just!

We give you thanks, O God, through your beloved Child Jesus Christ, whom you have sent us in the last days as Savior, Redeemer, and Messenger of your will. He is your Word, inseparable from you, through whom you have created everything and in whom you find your delight. You sent him from heaven into the womb of a Virgin. He was conceived and became flesh, he manifested himself as your Son, born of the Spirit and the Virgin. He did your will, and, to win for you a holy people, he stretched out his hands in suffering to rescue from suffering those who believe in you.

When he was about to surrender himself to voluntary suffering in order to destroy death, to break the devil's chains, to tread hell underfoot, to pour out his light upon the just, to establish the covenant, and manifest his resurrection, he took bread, gave you thanks and said: "Take, eat, this is my body which is broken for you." In like manner for the cup, he said: "This is my blood which is poured out for you. When you do this, do (it) it memory of me."

Remembering therefore your death and your resurrection, we offer you the bread and the wine, we thank you for having judged us worthy to stand before you and serve you.

And we pray you to send your Holy Spirit on the offering of your holy Church, to bring together in unity all those who receive it. May they be filled with the Holy Spirit who strengthens their faith in the truth. May we be able thus to praise and glorify you through your Child Jesus Christ.

Through him glory to you and honor, to the Father and the Son, with the Holy Spirit, in your holy Church, now and for ever and ever! Amen.

The Apostolic Tradition by St. Hippolytus

16

"make the eucharist." This invitation to invoke the wonders of God has antecedents in the Jewish liturgy, but here its formulation is distinctly christological: the wonder evoked is the creative and redemptive work of the incarnate Word whose death and resurrection is the world's salvation. Everything is presented in terms of giving thanks, a motif that appears again in the anamnesis and also underlies the final formula: the whole prayer is "eucharist."

The mention of the Last Supper is inserted in the course of the text, but the prayer is addressed to God the Father. The institution account is very sober, restricts itself to essentials, and witnesses an oral tradition that is independent from the wording found in the Scriptures

The anamnesis is linked to Christ's command to "Do this in memory of me," and mentions the Lord's death and resurrection. Through it the church presents to God the sacrifice of the Son made present in the sacrament: "Remembering . . . we offer." Everything is stated in one sentence, like a single element, in strict unity with the institution account.

The supplication follows immediately: it requests that the bread and wine become as a vehicle for the Spirit who will use them to bring forth fruits in those who receive them. The final trinitarian praise or doxology invites the "Amen" of the assembly.

From now on all eucharistic prayers will exhibit the same basic structure. Only the singing of the *Sanctus* and the intercessions will be added.

Another anaphora, which was written in Syria (in Syriac rather than Greek), and which is closely related to the Jewish tradition of table prayer, is certainly just as ancient, but it no longer remains frozen in the third century, since it is still used today in the liturgy. It appears in two different forms: the Maronites call it the third anaphora of St. Peter; the Eastern Syrians know it as the anaphora of Addai and Mari. We cannot completely reconstruct its original form. It is, however, addressed to Christ—an undeniable sign of its ancient character. The institution narrative appears in only one of the two contemporary witnesses to this prayer, and there it is combined with the anamnesis.

Concelebration

When we ask whether or not ancient practices correspond to our present definition of concelebration, it must be said that the principle of the one altar is observed, a principle still followed today by most of the Eastern Churches. In the *Apostolic Tradition* we find priests surrounding the bishop and extending their hands over the bread and wine with him; the

Prayer of Intercession, Anamnesis, and Institution Account in a Maronite Anaphora

Therefore, O Lord, on account of your many mercies, you make a gracious memorial for all the upright and just fathers in the commemoration of your body and blood which we offer to you upon your living and holy altar as you, our hope, have taught us in your holy gospel and have said: "I am the bread of life which came down from heaven so that mortals may have life in me."

O Lord, we make the memorial of your passion as you have taught us. In that night when you were delivered up to those who crucified you, O Lord, you took bread in your pure and holy hands, and you looked to heaven to your glorious Father. You blessed, signed, and sanctified it, O Lord, and broke and gave it to your disciples, the blessed apostles, and said to them, "This is my body which is broken and given for the life of the world, and for those who take it, for the pardon of debts and forgiveness of sins. Take, eat it, and it will be eternal life for you."

And likewise over the cup you gave thanks, O Lord, and glorified, and said, "This cup is my blood of the New Testament which is shed for many for the remission of sins. Take, drink from it, all of you, and it will be for the pardon of your debts and for the forgiveness of sins and eternal life. Amen.

For whenever you eat of this holy body and drink from this cup of life and salvation, you remember the death and resurrection of your Lord until "the great day" of his coming.

We remember your death, O Lord, your resurrection we proclaim, and we await the great day of your return. Have mercy on us all.

Third Anaphora of St. Peter

18

action is communal; the words are said by the presider alone. The *Teaching of the Apostles*, written about the same time yet in a completely different setting, speaks of the bishop's welcoming of a colleague from another country by having him say the thanksgiving or, should he refuse this honor, by inviting him to pronounce the words over the cup. There is no other witness to such a practice, but it supposes that the two celebrants offer one sacrifice, exercising one and the same priestly ministry.

This text recalls an anecdote related by St. Irenaeus: in the second century, the bishop of Rome and the bishop of Smyrna had some differences of opinion in regard to the date for celebrating Easter. Nonetheless, the pope—the bishop of Rome—yielded the presidency of the eucharist to his guest so as to manifest their communion. It is evident that they do not say the sacramental formulas together, since these texts do not as yet exist in fixed form.

* * * *

The Mass has its origins in the Last Supper. Yet Christ's words over the bread and the wine—"This is my body . . . This is my blood"—are what

---

Two Bishops Celebrate the Same Eucharist

. . . Irenaeus adds an account which I can relate:

And when the blessed Polycarp was at Rome in the time of Anicetus, and they disagreed a little about certain other things, they immediately made peace with one another, not caring to quarrel over this matter. For neither could Anicetus persuade Polycarp not to observe what he had always observed with John the disciple of our Lord, and the other apostles with whom he had associated; neither could Polycarp persuade Anicetus to observe it, as he said that he ought to follow the customs of the presbyters that had preceded him. But though matters were in this shape, they communed together, and Anicetus conceded the administration of the eucharist in the church to Polycarp, manifestly as a mark of respect. And they parted from each other in peace . . .

Eusebius of Caesarea, Church History, V 24. 16

we most frequently remember about this meal. This isolation of the words of the institution narrative risks transforming it into a quasi-magical formula. In reality, Jesus' words are part of a whole, part of a ritual action carried out in prayer: "Jesus gave thanks." If we neglect this setting, we cannot understand how the Mass came into existence. Having assumed its definitive shape as early as the middle of the second century, the Mass will subsequently undergo various evolutions. In its deepest being, however, it will be faithful to this shape in all ages.

Further Reading

Robert Cabié, *The Eucharist* 7-29.

Cheslyn Jones, Geoffrey Wainwright, and Edward Yarnold, eds., *The Study of Liturgy* (New York: Oxford University Press, 1978) 39-53, 147-176.

Joseph A. Jungmann, *The Mass of the Roman Rite* (1 volume edition) 3-18.

Jerome Kodell, *The Eucharist in the New Testament* (Wilmington, DE: Michael Glazier, 1988).

Willy Rordorf and others, *The Eucharist of the Early Christians*, tr. Matthew J. O'Connell (New York: Pueblo Publishing Company, 1978).

Chapter II

Mass in the Basilicas
IV- VIII century

The fourth century witnesses a new stage in the history of the Mass. This evolution is not, as so many seem to think, the result of the Edict of Toleration in the year 313, though Constantine's decree did encourage and hasten this development by ensuring that the number of Christians would continue to increase.

Basilicas

The earliest Christians gathered for the eucharist in individual homes; the more well-to-do among the faithful placed at the disposal of the church rooms that, as often as possible, were used exclusively for worship. Contrary to popular belief, the catacombs were never places for regular worship during the period of the persecutions. Because cemeteries were open to the public, they could not be used as hiding places. The sacrifice of the Lord was celebrated in the catacombs only on the anniversary of a person's death when people desired to pray at the tombs of the deceased.

In the third century some communities, having obtained enough wealth, purchased ordinary houses and arranged them according to their needs: an example is Dura-Europos on the Euphrates, whose ruins antedate the year 256. Not until the end of the century were buildings constructed expressly to house the liturgical assembly, a need that increased rapidly after the Peace of Constantine. Architects could not draw their inspiration from the temples, which were dwelling places of the various gods; and whose main sections, containing the divine statue or symbols, were small in size, even

21

Empereur Alexander Severus (222-235) Arbitrates

The Christians were occupying an old vacant building; the tavern keepers, however, were opposed to this because it belonged to them. He [the emperor] decided that it would be better that a god, of whatever sort, be adored there rather than to use the building for the sale of drink.

Lampridus, Life of Alexander Severus 6

The Assembly in a House, in 304

[The proconsul of Carthage questions a reader named Emeritus]

— It is indeed in your house that the gathering takes place, contrary to the decrees of the emperors?
— It is in my house that we hold the assembly of the Lord.
— Why have you allowed them to enter there?
— Because they are my brothers and I was unable to forbid them.
— But you were supposed to have forbidden them.
— I could not do so because we cannot exist without the assembly of the Lord.

Acts of the Martyrs of Abitene

when surrounded by open spaces or colonnades. Christians needed "houses of the people," because the people themselves are the Lord's true dwelling place made of living stones. So the church had recourse to basilicas, namely, those public buildings that served as places where justice was administered, where public gatherings were held, and where all social transactions took place. ("Basilica" comes from the Greek *basilikos* which means "imperial.") Rectangular in form with prominent roofs, basilicas were generally divided by a double or a quadruple row of columns into three or five naves (interior spaces or halls). At one end, often at the far end of the apse (a semi-circular, projecting space, often under a dome), was the chair for the judge or magistrate. It was easy to adapt such a space for liturgical purposes.

The Greek word *ecclesia*, meaning a "gathering," was also applied to the meeting place. The rites had to be adapted to these larger spaces: if the

A Church in Syria in the Fifth Century

This is how a church is to be arranged: there will be three entrances in honor of the Trinity. The sacristy (*diakonikon*) will be to the right of the right entrance, so that the eucharists, namely, the gifts that are brought, can be seen. The sacristy will have a forward area surrounded by a portico. A baptistry is to be placed here.

The church will have an area for the catechumens, also to be used by the door-keepers. This place will not be separate from the church so that [the catechumens] might enter the church and remain there to hear the readings, the spiritual canticles, and the psalms. A bench will be placed close to the altar, to the right and to the left [to serve as] seating places for the priests in such a way that those who are more elevated [in dignity] and more honorable might sit on the right with those who carry the word, whereas the middle-aged sit on the left. The bench will be elevated by three degrees: likewise for the altar which should be located there.

The building will have two porches, one on the right for the men and another on the left for the women. . .

The Testament of Our Lord 1. 19

essential actions of the celebration were to remain prominent, they had to be expanded. That is, the rites had to borrow new forms of expression from the customs of secular society, namely, from the protocol of the court or the government.

Major Liturgical Families

Liturgical developments necessarily entailed various forms according to the culture of each region; and major liturgical families were formed under the influence of the most prestigious episcopal cities. In the East various zones of influence were gradually organized: Jerusalem adapted itself to the needs of the pilgrims coming to it; Antioch served West Syrian, Byzantine, Armenian, Georgian, and Maronite populations; the East Syrians lived beyond the frontiers of the Empire, and the great city of Alexandria was a center for the Copts and later for the Ethiopians. Only three of the episcopal cities in the West developed liturgical rites that are still important to us: the liturgy of Rome is still celebrated throughout the world; Milan gave us the Ambrosian Rite; and the Hispanic tradition, which resembles the Gallican rites, survives in the city of Toledo. Thus were the external forms of the celebration of Mass enriched and diversified without any rejection of the heritage of the first centuries. It is our common acceptance of this heritage that assures the complete unity of the Mass amid this great diversity.

Various Forms of the Eucharistic Prayer

To get some idea of this diversity, we will consider the eucharistic prayer, the words said over the bread and wine from the preface to the communion rite. In the East, the churches used a variety of formularies, each one having a fixed form from beginning to end. Rome, on the other hand, had only one eucharistic prayer, commonly called the Canon of the Mass, but this text contained variable sections. The most important variable section occurred at the beginning: only one motive for giving thanks was evoked each time, but its formulation changed according to the days and seasons of the year. The most ancient, though partial, version of the Roman Canon has been found at Milan, apparently from the hand of the bishop Ambrose. On the other hand, in Gaul and Spain only the words of Jesus at the Last Supper, the institution narrative, was invariable: the prayers preceding and following it differed from celebration to celebration.

The stylistic originality imparted by local cultures cannot be overlooked. The precision, brevity, and sobriety that we now see in the Roman texts reflect a civilization that was strongly influenced by jurists. By contrast, the liturgical language of Spain or Gaul was verbose, sometimes poetic, with repeating themes and many parallel phrases. Byzantine texts, on the other hand, were often expanded into beautiful literary constructions, whereas the prayer of the East Syrians remained faithful to Semitic tradition and appeared as a succession of small connected units.

Participation by the People

Everywhere the Mass was celebrated, the people fully participated, under the presidency of the bishop surrounded by his priests. Indeed, they expressed such abundant enthusiasm at times that it was difficult to control

---

The Canon at Milan at the Time of St. Ambrose

The priest speaks. He says: "Perform for us this oblation written, reasonable, acceptable, which is a figure of the body and blood of our Lord Jesus Christ. On the day before he suffered He took bread in His holy hands, looked toward heaven, toward you, holy Father omnipotent, eternal God, giving thanks, blessed, broke, and having broken gave it to the Apostles and His disciples saying: 'Take and eat of this, all of you; for this is my body, which shall be broken for many'." Take note. "Similarly also, on the day before He suffered, after they had dined, He took the chalice, looked toward heaven, toward thee, holy Father omnipotent, eternal God and giving thanks He blessed it, and gave it to the Apostles and His disciples, saying: 'Take and drink of this, all of you; for this is my blood'." . . . He says: "As often as you shall do this, so often will you do a commemoration of me, until I come again." And the priest says: "Therefore, mindful of His most glorious passion and resurrection from the dead and ascension into heaven, we offer you this immaculate victim, a reasonable sacrifice, an unbloody victim, this holy bread, and chalice of eternal life. And we ask and pray that you accept this offering upon your sublime altar through the hands of your angels, just as you deigned to accept the gifts of your just son Abel and the sacrifice of our patriarch Abraham and what the highest priest Melchisedech offered you."

Ambrose, On the Sacraments IV 5-6

An Extract from a Hispanic Eucharistic Prayer

O Lord, we make memory of your Son . . . coming among us, he took upon himself the human condition; to ransom those whom he had created, he endured the passion of the cross for the salvation of all; to conquer and trample underfoot the death we have merited, he handed himself over to a death he did not merit; he partially stripped hell, abandoning there the impious and having the holy ones held there go up with him, at the time of his resurrection, into heaven; returning to heaven, he opened for us the way to attain heaven; he will come to judge the living and the dead, to condemn criminals and sinners to eternal punishment, and to restore to his faithful the glory of his eternity. It is through him, Father most high, that we ask you to receive kindly this offering which is worthy of pleasing you, an offering we present with our hands; we ask that you, from your throne in heaven, bless and look favorably upon it so that all of us, who will receive part of it as food, might draw from it salvation and the healing of soul and body.

The Book of Masses from Toledo, Fourth Sunday of Advent,"Post Pridie"

the gathering. The deacons, who never sat so that they might better ensure the service of the sanctuary and the animation of the common prayer, directed everyone's participation in the celebration; readers proclaimed the Scriptures from the ambo (or lectern); soloists (cantors) and choir sang (in alternation) psalms, hymns, or tropes (embellishments) with the assistance of all the faithful.

Ministers, distinguished by the places they occupied in the assembly, wore no distinctive vestments. Nevertheless, they did try to choose garments that differed, not by their cut but by their beauty, from those worn on the street. The historical period we are studying saw the appearance of several distinctive styles, at times borrowed from the Roman and Byzantine court ceremonial; yet it was fidelity to a long garment, considered more dignified when fashion substituted other garb, that gave rise to liturgical vesture.

During this period, the language of the liturgy was understood by all Christians, though it was sometimes necessary to rely on extemporaneous translations of the readings, prayers, homilies, and admonitions, since the assembly was not always homogenous and because, after invasions or other migrations, the texts no longer existed in the local language.

Until this time the only liturgical book was the Bible. But the prayers handed down through oral tradition were soon written down and circulated from one community to another; provincial councils carefully oversaw this

A Multilingual Assembly at Jerusalem

A portion of the population in this province knows both Greek and Syriac; another segment knows only Greek; and still another, only Syriac. Even though the bishop may know Syriac, he always speaks Greek and never Syriac; and, therefore, there is always present a priest who, while the bishop speaks in Greek, translates into Syriac so that all may understand what is being explained. Since whatever scriptural texts are read must be read in Greek, there is always someone present who can translate the readings into Syriac for the people, so that they will always understand. So that those here who are Latins, those consequently knowing neither Greek nor Syriac, will not be bored, everything is explained to them, for there are other brothers and sisters who are bilingual in Greek and Latin and who explain everything to them in Latin.

Egeria, Diary of a Pilgrim, Chapter 47

Variety of Customs and Frequency of the Eucharist

Some receive daily the Body and Blood of the Lord, others receive it on certain days; in some places no day is omitted in the offering of the Holy Sacrifice, in others it is offered only on Saturday and Sunday, or even only on Sunday; and as to other such differences as may be noted, there is freedom in all these matters, and there is no better rule for the earnest and prudent Christian than to act as he sees the Church act wherever he is staying.

Augustine, Letter 54 to Januarius

No Mass on Feast Days in Rural Areas

Should anyone desire to build a chapel in the country-side—apart from parishes where the legitimate and ordinary assembly is held--we grant permission for this. We are favorably disposed to do so by reason of the hardship of the people who come there; Mass may be celebrated in these chapels except on feasts. On Easter, Christmas, Epiphany, the Lord's Ascension, Pentecost, and the Nativity of St. John the Baptist, and on great feast days, Mass will only be celebrated in cities and in parishes. Clerics celebrating Mass in chapels without the mandate or permission of the bishop will be excommunicated.

Council of Agde in 506, Canon 21

development to avoid unorthodox or untraditional formulations. Some bishops composed or reworked formulas for use in their own churches, and these in turn were disseminated in small "fascicles" or *libelli* (small booklets). Eventually these scattered notes were gathered together in more complete collections, some of which were perfected or somewhat perfected, at the beginning of the sixth century.

Each minister could, therefore, possess his own book. In the West, the presider's book is called the sacramentary; in the East, it is known as the euchologium (because it contains the eucharistic prayers). The oldest Roman sacramentary that has come down to us—incorrectly called the *leonine sacramentary* after Pope Leo—is a simple, unorganized collection of *libelli* that were gathered together to be imitated and conserved. Gradually, however, other books were formed to provide for each celebration of the liturgical year, and two traditions appear. The first, called the "gregorian," is used for papal celebrations; the other, known as the "gelasian," is used by presbyters.

The reader used a Bible in which were indicated—by a series of marginal notes or through an appendix—the readings assigned to a particular day. Such notations were especially required when the continuous reading was interrupted for special celebrations, as was frequently the case. The Gospels, which were always proclaimed by a deacon, were contained in a special volume, more richly bound and illustrated. In addition, books were prepared for use by the cantors, and also, much later, the *Ordo* appeared, which described how the ceremonies were to be carried out.

Masses during the Week
and the Creation of New Places for Worship

In the beginning the eucharist was celebrated only on Sunday. The first exception to this rule, perhaps occurring at the end of the second century, was the addition of the day on which a martyr's death was commemorated at his or her tomb. Not until the fourth century do we find other celebrations of the eucharist occurring during the week—after which the practice grew rapidly, especially in the West. Nonetheless, except for certain churches, for example, Hippo at the time of Augustine, and other localized cases, Mass was never celebrated daily; in fact this practice has never become universally obligatory. In the East, references to Mass on Saturday became frequent during this period; and the reasons given for this development were clearly separate from the Jewish observance of the Sabbath. In any case, the priest was always considered as presiding "over the assembly," no matter the day or the size of the gathering.

Often enough the presider was a presbyter, or ordained priest, other than the bishop. In urban areas and as the number of Christians increased, it becomes necessary to construct basilicas in addition to the bishop's: thus at Rome "titular" or neighborhood churches were built. And once the countryside was evangelized, parishes are created in the more important areas; in fact, oratories or small private chapels were constructed on the property of the more prominent landowners. This proliferation of buildings did, and continues to do, violence to the principle that the (local) church is one assembly at which the bishop of the diocese presides. In the beginning, certainly, there was an attempt to minimize this disadvantage: the Roman "titular" churches were not parishes; as the liturgical year unfolded, each church became in turn a place or "station" at which the eucharist would be celebrated; the pope presided at the liturgy and people from all sections of the city were represented. Nevertheless, some alternatives had to be provided for those unable to participate at the stational church.

In rural areas, especially Gaul (in west and central Europe) for which the most testimony exists, new parishes were only created gradually, and permission was granted to celebrate the eucharist on Sunday on farming estates or in "villas," but this permission did not apply to the major feasts of the year. On great feastdays, everyone went to the cathedral for the bishop's Mass. Local church councils, however, progressively reduced the number of these feasts until finally only the presence of the leading citizens, those having the means to leave home, was required at the cathedral. The people's needs elicited these pastoral concessions, but history shows no desire or urgency to dismantle the unity of the diocesan church, whose essential sign was the eucharistic assembly.

From Constantine to Charlemagne

In the next two chapters we will follow the development of the liturgy from Constantine to Charlemagne. Bracketing the period between these two emperors is not only a convenient means of recalling dates; it also outlines the direction that liturgical evolution will follow—at least from a western perspective. We will occasionally do some injustice to this framework to include observations about eastern liturgical developments, but for clarity of presentation, we will remain in this historical mode as much as possible. Even though the rites of the Mass developed in a rather homogenous manner throughout this period, we will distinguish two steps.

First, we will consider the changes underway as early as the fourth century in all the churches of the Christian world, even if these developments are expressed differently in the various liturgical families. Then we will treat elements that are more specific to the Roman tradition, especially from the pontificate of Gelasius I (492-496) onward.

To summarize briefly our journey thus far: Liturgical development is a continuous movement whose various moments harmonize with one another. When Christians participate in the eucharist, they are indeed conscious of forming an assembly (even when the gathering is reduced in size) that influences the personal journey of each participant. The bishop or presbyter is first of all the person presiding over this assembly; his function is defined by this service, behind which his own feelings and piety give way. When he says the words, he always does so in a loud voice since he addresses the people or presents to God the prayer of all the faithful. The architectural space of the basilica—an open nave dominated by the episcopal chair, an ambo for proclaiming the word, and one altar—manifests the vision of the church expressed by the celebration.

Further Reading

Robert Cabié, *The Eucharist* 36-40.

Peter Fink, "Traditions, Liturgical, in the East," in *The New Dictionary of Sacramental Worship* (Collegeville: The Liturgical Press, 1990) 1255-1272.

Cheslyn Jones and others, eds., *The Study of Liturgy* 179-188.

Theodor Klauser, *A Short History of the Western Liturgy* 140-146.

T.F. Mathews, "Church Architecture. 2. Early Christian," *New Catholic Encyclopedia*, vol. 3, 775-779,

Robert Taft, "The Frequency of the Eucharist throughout History" in *Beyond East and West: Problems in Liturgical Understanding* (Washington, D.C.: The Pastoral Press, 1984) esp. 61-66.

Chapter III

"The Holy Mysteries"
IV - V century

As we look carefully at the basic structure of the Mass in the fourth and fifth centuries, we see the same fundamental pattern appearing in all the churches and the same meaning applying to the various parts of the celebration. But we also discover a variety of practices that, like a many-colored garment, highlight the abundant richness of the Mass.

Entering the Celebration

Though Justin's description indicated that the Mass began with the readings, he had also insisted that all Christians meet together in the same place, and it was this insistence that gave rise to the introductory rites. The first of these rites to appear was the greeting, then the entrance song, and the opening prayer.

The people were already in the basilica when the bishop entered: he passed through the multitude of the faithful and, having reached his chair, greeted everyone in the name of Jesus: "Peace be to you," "Peace be to all," "The Lord be with you." The response is the same everywhere: "And with your spirit." This Semitic formula could also have been correctly translated as "And to you," or, "and with you." Yet the words were not so understood. Instead people saw here an allusion to the Spirit received through the laying on of hands at ordination. The assembly gathered in response to God's call; it gathered as an image of the Body whose head is Christ. This unity of Christ and the faithful and this presence of Christ in

Easter Sunday in 426: The Mass Begins at Hippo

(A young man, afflicted with tremblings, has just been miraculously cured.)

We advanced toward the people. The church was full and resonated with cries of joy: Glory to God! Praise to God! No one was quiet, and the cries arose from all part. I greeted the people who again cried out, redoubling their enthusiasm. When silence was finally restored, the readings of the Sacred Scriptures were proclaimed. When the moment came for me to speak, I said a few words related to the solemnity and to the joy which penetrated, leaving the faithful to admire the eloquence of God in the work which he had just accomplished rather than my discourse.

Augustine, The City of God 22. 8. 22

"And with your Spirit"

The people respond to the priest with love as they say: With you, O priest, and with the sacerdotal spirit you possess! They say that the "spirit" and not the "soul" is in the priest, since it is the Spirit which the priest has received through the imposition of hands. By this imposition the priest receives the Spirit through which he becomes capable of carrying out the Mysteries . . . May the peace of your spirit increase by reason of your diligence in spiritual things.

Narsai of Nisbis, Homily 1

34

Church is the meaning of the sacramental presidency of the priest; his ministry is not a human honor but a service.

Often enough people continued to chat among themselves when these first words were spoken. But before long a psalm was introduced to unite all voices, to form a people through whose midst God's minister walked forward. Often, as at Rome, this psalm was used with an antiphon or choral response to create the tone or climate for the feast or the liturgical season; or, as happened in the East, another chant was used for this purpose, the very popular "Holy God, Strong One, Immortal One, have mercy on us," which, in Gaul, was sung in both Greek and Latin.

This solemn entrance of the liturgical minister included an enthronement of the Book of the Gospels, which was carefully and prominently placed on the altar. From the earliest times of biblical revelation God's word had united and symbolized the people of the covenant. The Byzantines so developed this feature that it came to overshadow all the other elements and became known as the "Little Entrance," or entrance of the "Book."

From the moment it was formed, the assembly turned to God the Father in the harmony of its various functions; we find this in the Roman liturgy's opening prayer with its four parts: the invitation (let us pray), supplication in silence, the "collect," and the *Amen*. The "collect" as its name implies is the gathering up and summation of the people's supplications in a formal presidential prayer. Through the "Amen," each member of the assembly joined his or her individual prayers to that of the other participants, to that of the church speaking through the voice of its minister, to that of Christ himself whose mediation was thus invoked ("Through Jesus Christ, your Son").

Proclamation of the Word

A reader then ascended to the ambo, that is, to an elevated lectern from which he or she could be clearly seen and heard. Often the reader was a child, whose voice carried better in the large space of the basilica. In Syria the pulpit was located on a platform erected in the middle of the nave; here the clergy gathered for the first part of the Mass.

Ordinarily the first reading was a passage from the Old Testament; then a soloist sang a psalm; after each strophe the assembly responded, echoing the word that, having touched their hearts, ascends to God. Another reader then proclaimed the "apostle": an extract from one of the epistles, the Acts of the Apostles, or the Book of Revelation. A deacon next came forward, carrying the book of the gospels that he had earlier placed on the altar; meanwhile the *Alleluia* continued to resound between verses of a psalm.

35

Thus was the assembly brought to a high point: everything hereafter will be more solemn. At this point in churches with seating, everyone stood. "Wisdom! Stand! Be attentive!" cried out the deacon in the Byzantine rite. This pattern, depending on the rite and the liturgical day, could easily be expanded by inserting additional readings from the Old or New Testament, but it could also be reduced to a single reading before the gospel.

The Reader Makes a Mistake

It was a short psalm which we had prepared and asked the reader to sing. But the reader, undoubtedly troubled at the last moment, made a mistake and took another. As for us, we prefer to follow God's will in this mistake of the reader rather than our own will in regard to what we had chosen. If, then, we hold you longer because of the length of this psalm, do not reproach us, but rather think that it is always with fruit that God wishes to have us work.

Augustine, Commentary on Psalm 139

Next, the presider offered his intervention. His homily, like that of Jesus in the synagogue at Nazareth, was an announcement: "Today this scripture passage is fulfilled in your hearing" (Lk 4:21). The homily was always a familiar type of speech in which literary pretensions had to give way to the listeners' need to understand. Augustine, for example, did not hesitate to use words from the Berber dialect; nor did he hesitate to provoke reactions from the assembly.

The General Intercessions

The universal prayer (or general intercessions) were the prerogative of the faithful, namely, those who had received the sacraments of Christian initiation. The *Apostolic Tradition* is an early witness of this fact: the neophytes (the newly baptized), having left the baptistery, returned to the assembly and participated in this prayer for the first time. By so doing they accepted their share in the priestly mission of Christ who had devoted his life to the salvation of the world.

By contrast, the catechumens who, of course, were not yet baptized, had to leave the assembly before this prayer began. At Antioch the faithful prayed for those who were to be dismissed (the catechumens); these in turn were blessed before a deacon gave them notice to leave the church. An order following their dismissal directed that the doors of the church be closed. The general intercessions were then prayed by the faithful who alone remained in the church.

In the East, the litany was the most popular form of this prayer. A deacon announced a series of intentions, each followed by a resounding *Kyrie eleison*, which the people addressed to Christ. This model was imitated by some of the western churches, for example, those of Milan, Ireland, and Gaul.

At Rome the form of this prayer was more solemn, as we can see from the form that is still used today on Good Friday. A series of petitions was offered having the following structure. First was an invitation to pray, followed by a moment of silence (during penitential seasons the people knelt). This formula appears to be the oldest part of this rite. It was followed by a prayer of supplication concluded by the *Amen* of the assembly. Was such a pattern followed in Egypt? A fourth-century Egyptian prayer book contains three presidential prayers: for the fruitfulness of the earth, for the sick, and for the bishop and the community.

Presentation of the Gifts

The bread and the cup were brought forward to the president of the assembly. Justin had already referred to this moment, and in the third century Hippolytus indicated that it was the deacons who performed this service. But a new element appeared during this time: from their own tables at home, the faithful brought gifts to the church—materials for the eucharist. In this way they expressed their participation in the sacrifice, something the catechumens were unable to do, and thus they expected its fruits to apply to their own intentions.

At Rome and in Africa, the faithful formed a procession with their gifts—as they would later form a procession for communion—and proceeded to the sanctuary after the general intercessions. Augustine saw in

> ### The Offering of the Poor Benefits the Communion of the Rich
>
> You are well-off and rich, and you believe that you celebrate the Lord's Supper . . . when you come without an offering and receive part of the offering brought by a person who is needy. Consider the widow in the Gospel . . .
>
> *Cyprian, Concerning Works and Almsgiving 15*

The Offering of a Blind Man
Who Was Miraculously Cured

The man who had been blind went toward the altar . . . according to custom to present the offering for his cure . . . and the bishop received it and placed it on the altar.

Victor of Vita, The Persecution by the Vandals II. 17

A Lively Offertory Procession in Gaul

It was the feast of St. Polycarp the martyr, and there was a solemn celebration at Rion, a suburb of the city of Arvernes. After the passion of the saint and the other readings prescribed by the rules of the church were proclaimed, it was time to offer the sacrifice. Having taken the "tower" [a liturgical vessel imitating the tomb of Christ in Jerusalem] containing the sacrament ["mysterium"] of the body of the Lord, the deacon began to carry it to the door of the church which he entered to place it on the altar. But the vessel flew out of his hands and, floating through the air, it arrived at the altar without the deacon being able to catch it. In my opinion, the only reason for this was that the deacon's conscience was charged with sin.

Gregory of Tours, The Book of Miracles to the Glory of the Martyrs

this action the "admirable exchange" of the incarnation: Christ receives his humanity from us that he might give us his divinity. The action is accompanied by the singing of a psalm.

Elsewhere, the offerings were placed in the sacristy before the celebration, and the deacons brought them solemnly to the altar at the beginning of the liturgy of the eucharist. In Gaul, the details of this custom are known

A Widow Offers for Her Spouse

In this city [Lyons] lived two people who belonged to the senatorial class, a man and a woman, without children, who at the end of their lives left all their goods to the church. The husband, after he died, was buried in the basilica of Sancta Maria. Throughout the year his wife attended this church where she prayed assiduously; each day she participated in the celebration of Mass for which she offered, in memory of her husband, a pint of Gaza wine, which she brought to the sacristy of the holy basilica. She did not doubt that God's mercy would grant peace to her deceased husband on the day when she presented the offering to the Lord for his soul. But a good-for-nothing subdeacon, keeping the Gaza wine for his own use, put as an offering into the chalice some very bitter wine [availing himself of the fact that] the woman did not always receive communion.

But God was pleased to reveal the fraud. The husband appeared in a dream to his wife and said to her: "Tell me, dear spouse, why have I worked so hard in this world, only now to receive weak wine for an offering?" But she replied: "Truly, I have not forgotten your love, and it is always Gaza wine, and the best of it, that I bring for your rest to the sacristy of my God." Upon awakening, the widow, greatly troubled by this vision and unable to forget it, arose for the morning office as was her custom. But at the Mass which was afterwards celebrated, she approached the drink of salvation. From the chalice she drank wine which was so bitter that she believed it would pull out her teeth, as she swallowed this strange drink. Then, inveighing against the subdeacon, she demanded reparation for the harm done by his maliciousness.

Gregory of Tours, The Book of Miracles to the Glory of Confessors

to us only through more recent witnesses. Their practice was similar, however, to the procession of the gifts in the eastern rites, which, beginning at the end of the sixth century, underwent a magnificent expansion and became the rite of the "Great Entrance" with the singing of Cherubim's hymn. Each of these patterns anticipated the reality the gifts would become in the eucharistic prayer: indeed, everything about the presentation of the gifts calls to mind a procession with the blessed sacrament.

> **The Hymn of the Cherubim**
>
> We who mystically represent the cherubim and sing the thrice-holy hymn to the life-giving Trinity, let us lay aside all worldly care to receive the King of all, escorted unseen by the angelic corps.
>
> *Byzantine Liturgy, Hymn at the "Great Entrance"*

For the conclusion of the offertory, the priest was at the altar. This part of the celebration was above all an action; the only words spoken were those that concluded it. In the Roman rite it was the prayer over the gifts, a brief formula at the end of the psalm, just as the collect is found at the end of the entrance psalm. In other liturgies (for example, those of Gaul and Spain) the names of those who had contributed the gifts for the eucharist were read. Then, in a presidential oration called the *Post nomina* ("After the names"), mention was made of the living and the dead who were to be remembered.

The Eucharistic Prayer

Now we have arrived at the anaphora. Its basic structure has already been attested by the *Apostolic Tradition*: the expression of thanksgiving, the institution account and the anamnesis, the request that the communicants receive the fruits of the Mass, the doxology, and the assembly's *Amen*. And yet, in addition to the various forms of this prayer that were already mentioned in Chapter 2, developments occurred in the fourth and fifth centuries that were almost the same everywhere: the introduction of the *Sanctus*, the expansion of the request concerning the communion, the addition of intercessions.

"Holy, holy, holy Lord, God of heaven . . ." This hymn, taken from the vision in which Isaiah was called (Is 6:3), was sung at the morning office in the synagogue, not as part of the table liturgy, which perhaps explains why it did not appear in the eucharist until now. The *Sanctus* was introduced by citing the heavenly liturgy, though this introduction was sometimes rather poorly connected with the context immediately preceding it. Heaven was always added to the text from Isaiah because it, like the earth, is *full* of God's glory. The Egyptian and Ethiopian prayers repeated this word as they continued: "*Fill* also this sacrifice with the power of your Spirit," thus introducing the *epiclesis*, the request or "calling down" of the Spirit on these gifts to make them holy. At Rome the Spirit was not explicitly named, but the presider continued: "Bless and approve our offering: make it acceptable to you, an offering in spirit and in truth. Let it become for us the body and blood of Jesus Christ, your only Son, our Lord."

All traditions, except that of Alexandria, completed the citation from Isaiah with an acclamation taken from the Gospel: "Blessed is he who comes in the name of the Lord. Hosanna in the highest" (Mt 21:9; cf. Ps 17:26). The idea of "holiness" symbolized in the *Sanctus* was often taken up again at the institution account with the words: "Truly, holy is the Lord . . . who, on the eve of his passion . . ."

Toward the conclusion of the anaphora found in the *Apostolic Tradition*, is yet another request that the Spirit come upon the gifts, so that those who receive communion will also receive the fruits of the eucharist. As the theology of the third person of the Trinity deepened in the East, the first part of this request took on the form of an *epiclesis* asking that the Spirit come upon the bread and the wine so that they become the body and blood of Christ. The sanctification of those who received the eucharist was indeed the result of the consecration, the work of the Spirit. The Roman Canon does not mention the Holy Spirit, but through the image of the two altars heaven and earth, it sketches out a double movement: our offerings ascend toward God and are returned with blessings on those who approach the eucharistic table.

Intercessory prayers enriched this supplication, expressed ecclesial communion around the altar, and recommended to God those who participate in the offering. A sign of the late introduction of these prayers can be seen in the variety of their positions in the various liturgical rites: at the end of the anaphora in the Antiochene rites; before the *Sanctus* in the Alexandrine tradition; some after the *Sanctus* and some toward the end of the Canon in the Roman tradition. The intercessions were lacking only in Gaul and in Spain where, as we have already mentioned, the names were read after the offertory before the eucharistic prayer.

Reading the Names of Those Who Offer?

The names of those who offer are now read aloud, and the redemption of sinners is turned toward their own praise; they no longer remember the widow of the Gospel who, by placing her two small coins in the treasury, surpassed all the offerings of the rich.

In the churches the deacon publicly proclaims the names of those who offer . . . and they offer themselves with delight to the applause of the people, while their consciences torture them.

Jerome, On Jeremiah II. 108 and On Ezekiel VI. 16

Epiclesis from the Byzantine Anaphora of St. Basil

Through the benevolence of your goodness, cause your Holy Spirit to come upon us and upon these gifts which we present to you, that he may bless them, sanctify them, and present to us in this bread the precious body and blood of Our Lord, God and Savior Jesus Christ, and in this cup the precious blood of Our Lord, God and Savior Jesus Christ, shed for the life of the world. And all of us who partake of the same bread and the same cup, unite us with one another in communion with the same Spirit. Cause that none of us partake in the sacred body and in the blood of your Christ unto judgment or condemnation, but so that we might find mercy and grace with all the saints that have been pleasing to you from the beginning of the ages.

A Pope Speaks about the "Fermentum"

As to the "fermentum" which we send on Sunday into the various titular churches, it is superfluous for you to consult us on this topic: here all the churches are built within the city. The priests of these churches, being unable to celebrate with us on this day because of the people entrusted to them, thus receive from the acolytes the "fermentum" confected by us so that they, especially on this day, do not feel separated from our communion.

Innocent I, Letter to Decentius Bishop of Gubbio (416)

The Breaking of the Bread,
the "Our Father," and the Kiss of Peace

As soon as the assembly's *Amen* resounds, the breaking of the bread followed nearly everywhere (except among the Byzantines who prayed the *Pater*, the Our Father, at this time as Rome will later). The bishop and the priests broke the bread. This action was strictly utilitarian, a preparation for the ministers and people's communion. At the same time, the action was also highly symbolic; in Jewish tradition the father of the family divided the bread for his household; Paul's comment remains vivid in our memories: "The bread that we break, is it not a participation in the body of Christ? Because the loaf of bread is one, we, though many, are one body, for we all partake of the one loaf" (1 Cor 10:16-17). This rite—the breaking of the bread—required a fair time to accomplish, and was always accorded a certain degree of solemnity.

A portion of the bread was placed in the cup. Was it that the bread that had been reserved for the sick at a previous Mass and now, having become stale, had to be consumed? Without a doubt. But at Rome it was also a sign of ecclesial unity. The bishop sent a portion of the eucharistic bread that he had consecrated to the priests who were celebrating Mass in the neighborhood churches; they place this portion in their own chalices. This particle is called the *fermentum*. Nevertheless, Rome's practice does not fully explain the universality of the rite. Surely the purpose of adding bread to the cup was to show that the Christ present in the sacrament is living today: if the body and blood being separated recall his death, so then their being joined recall his resurrection. This is also why the Byzantines pour some boiling water into the cup: the warmth of the chalice is another sign of life.

The Lord's Prayer, having always been considered a special preparation for communion, was now said: patristic commentaries on this prayer often extemporized on the request for "daily bread." If the obvious meaning of these words has nothing to do with the eucharist, we can still understand them, as Ambrose did, in a sacramental way. More often, however, the commentaries focus on the words "forgive us . . . as we forgive."

For this reason the Roman liturgy, as well as that of Africa, introduced the kiss of peace at this time, which, in the words of Tertullian, is "the seal placed upon the prayer." In other churches the faithful greeted one another before the eucharistic prayer or anaphora, when the gifts were brought forward. Their reason for doing so was the Lord's exhortation: "Therefore, if you bring your gift to the altar, and there recall that your brother has anything against you, leave your gift there at the altar, go first and be reconciled with your brother, and then come and offer your gift" (Mt 5:23-24).

The Communion

The presider was the first to receive the eucharist, then the clergy, and finally the other members of the faithful. Normally the bishop and the

The Body . . . the Blood of Christ. — Amen

So you say not indifferently "Amen," already confessing in spirit that you receive the body of Christ. Therefore, when you ask, the priest says to you: "the body of Christ," and you say: "Amen," that is, "truly." What the tongue confesses let the affection hold.

Ambrose, On the Sacraments V. 25

If you are the Body of Christ and his members, you are the sacrament of what is placed on the table of the Lord; it is the sacrament of what you are when you receive. It is to what you are that you respond "Amen." And this response is your signature. Be a member of the Body of Christ so that your Amen be true.

Augustine, Sermon 272

Receive Christ's Body in the Palm of Your Hand

So when you come come forward, do not come with arm extended or fingers parted. Make your left hand a throne for your right, since your right hand is about to welcome a king. Cup your palm and receive in it Christ's body, saying in response Amen. Then carefully bless your eyes with a touch of the holy body, and consume it, being careful to drop not a particle of it. For to lose any of it is clearly like losing part of your own body. Tell me, if anyone gave you some gold dust, would you not keep it with the greatest care, ensuring that you did not lose by dropping any part of it? So you should surely take still greater care not to drop a fragment of what is more valuable than gold and precious stones. After partaking of Christ's body, go to receive the chalice of his blood . . .

Cyril of Jerusalem: Mystagogical Catechesis V: 21

priests distributed the bread; the deacons presented the cup. The presence of the Lord can never be signified by things—even holy things—apart from a ministry confided to persons. John Chrysostom insists that the distribution of the eucharist is a service because it makes possible the following dialogue between the one who gives and the one who receives: "The body, the blood of Christ—Amen." Within a strongly communal context the interaction at communion is a highly personal act whereby faith in the eucharist is professed.

The faithful received the eucharist with hands placed one on the other; women covered their hands with a veil. They approached the altar while a psalm was being sung; in the East, frequently, Psalm 34 was used for communion: "Taste and see how good is the Lord"; at Rome more variety existed in the choice of this psalm.

The Concluding Rite

Generally the concluding rite consisted of a prayer followed by the deacon's dismissal of the assembly.

The core of the concluding rites in the Roman liturgy were two presidential prayers: the first, the postcommunion, requested the fruits of the eucharist; the second, the prayer over the people, asked for the Lord's blessings. The dismissal, *Ite, missa est*, is juridical in character, something akin to stating that "the meeting is adjourned." It had no properly religious content. Various other dismissals were used in the East, often "Go in peace," preceded by some other prayer formulas that differed from one church to another.

No singing whatever occurred during the people's departure.

Further Reading

Cheslyn Jones and others, eds., *The Study of Liturgy* 189-201.

Joseph A. Jungmann, *The Mass of the Roman Rite* (1 volume edition) 37-45.

Chapter IV

"Missarum sollemnia"
VI - VIII century

As indicated earlier, development in this new stage does not constitute a break with tradition; rather it comes as a culmination of the preceding evolutions. Churches exchanged with one another, borrowing, translating, and adapting—even crossing the frontiers that would later be closed by eastern opposition to the christological councils of the fifth century. Although we will take care not to overlook the riches found in this diversity of customs, we will allude to them only briefly. So that we do not stray too far afield, our primary focus will be on developments in the Roman tradition.

In its outward manifestation, the liturgy of this period resembled the ceremonial of the princely court. This development began with the pope's assumption of civic importance in the city when the Byzantine power proved ineffective in combating the assaults of the Barbarians. Masters of ceremonies, entrusted with the task of regulating the details of the liturgy, put together books of ceremonies to describe Roman customs. These books proved most useful when the liturgy had to be exported to regions unfamiliar with this tradition. The most important of these books for us is *Ordo Romanus I,* which in its earliest version undoubtedly dated from the end of the seventh century. This document will be our guide to the solemnities of the Mass, the *Missarum sollemnia.* As we study it, we will pay particular attention to elements that were changed during the two preceding centuries.

Entering the Basilica

Early in the morning the people gathered in the stational church at which the assembly was scheduled to take place. Bishops and priests sat on the bench that extends along the wall of the apse, the former to the right, the latter to the left of the presider's chair. The pope, escorted by dignitaries of the papal court, arrived on horseback from the Lateran palace. Greeted by the local clergy, he went first to the sacristy, which was usually surrounded with columns and located off the courtyard in front of the basilica. While the pope changed vestments, an acolyte carried the gospel book to the altar in the folds of his chasuble. He was accompanied by a subdeacon who carefully placed the book on the altar.

Once the pope has received the names of the readers and singers, the subdeacon of the region, standing at the entrance to the basilica, signaled the choir, or schola, to intone the psalm, which began with the antiphon of the day. The pope, assisted by two deacons, then entered the church. Preceding him were acolytes carrying seven candles and another subdeacon with an incense pan or censer. One of the honors accorded Roman magistrates was to be accompanied by incense as they went from place to place. The pontiff passed through the people, and through the two rows of the schola, at the front of the nave. Arriving at the altar, he gave a signal that they should begin the "Glory be to the Father." This doxology concluded the psalm, the sole function of which was to accompany the procession. The pope then spent a moment in silent prayer before going to his chair.

The Kyrie, the Gloria, and the Opening Prayer

The Greek *Kyrie eleison*—Lord have mercy, Christ have mercy, Lord have mercy—was now sung, with the pope indicating the number of times it was to be repeated. He then intoned: "Glory to God in the highest." These chants were new elements in the Mass, and though beautiful, they also delayed the dialogue of greeting between the presider and the gathering.

The *Kyrie* appeared as early as 529, when the Council of Vaison spoke of it as a "custom that is introduced in the Apostolic See as in all the other provinces of the east and west." It is difficult not to think of general intercessions here, that is, of the litany, the popular form of general prayer that Rome could have substituted for the more austere practice of admonitions and prayers mentioned in Chapter III. Pope Gelasius (492-496), moreover, composed a prayer of this type that was inspired by formularies from northern Italy. The text of one of these formularies has a Latin response (*Domine exaudi et miserere*, Hear us, O Lord, and have mercy),

The Prayer of Pope Gelasius

Let us all say: Hear us, O Lord, and have mercy upon us.

We call with faithful hearts upon the Father of the Only-begotten and upon the Spirit of God who is Creator from all eternity and upon God the Holy Spirit.

1. For an abundance of divine goodness upon the spotless church for the living God set up throughout the whole world.

2. For the holy priests of God the all-powerful, for the ministers of the sacred altar, and for all people who worship before the true God.

3. For all who are right bearers of the word of truth, we especially beg the manifold wisdom of him who is the Word of God.

4. For all those who mortify themselves in mind and body for the kingdom of heaven and busy themselves with the work of spiritual things, we beseech the Giver of spiritual gifts.

5. For holy rulers who hold in high esteem justice and right judgment and also for all the armies in their service, we call down the might of God.

6. For the comfort of good weather and suitable rains, for the careful tending of the vital winds and the favorable course of the seven seasons, we entreat the Lord and Governor of the world.

7. For those who by virtue of their initial acknowledgment of the Christian faith are now numbered among us and in whose hearts has been enkindled the burning desire for heavenly grace, we beg the mercy of almighty God.

8. For those caught in the weakness of human infirmity, who rejoice in sloth or in any other worldly error, we implore the mercy of our Redeemer.

9. For those undertaking long journeys or whom wicked powers have oppressed or the hardships of hostility have afflicted, we pray the Lord Our Savior.

10. For those deceived by Jewish error . . . or heretical perversity or steeped in pagan superstition, we beseech the Lord of truth.

11. For the doers of pious works, who out of fraternal charity care for the needs of the sick, we entreat the Lord of mercies.

12. For all who enter this holy house of the Lord and who gather here with religious fervor and suppliant devotion, we invoke the Lord of glory.

13. For the strength of our souls and bodies and for the forgiveness of all our sins, we beg the most merciful Lord.

14. For the repose of the faithful departed and especially for those holy priests of the Lord who have been in charge of this Catholic Church, we entreat the Lord of spirits and the Judge of all flesh . . .

Must Deacons Have a Beautiful Voice?

Some time ago, in this Roman Church, over which Divine Providence wished to place me, an exceedingly reprehensible custom arose. Certain chanters chosen for ministry at the sacred altar and ordained to the order of deacons that they might be devoted to sacred music, were called to the office of preaching and almsgiving. Whence it happens for many that while enticing duties draw you to the sacred ministry, a righteous life fails to attract. And the chanter, the minister, angers God by his manners while pleasing the people with his voice. Therefore, I establish by this decree from the (Apostolic) Chair that the sacred ministers ought not to sing and they may perform the office of reading the Gospel only during the solemnization of Masses; I decree that the psalms and other reading should be done by subdeacons, or if necessity requires it, by those in minor orders.

Gregory I, Roman Synod of 595

but it dates from the ninth century, and by that time an evolution may have occurred.

So why, then, was this piece moved to the entrance rites after the general prayer disappeared (sometime in the sixth century) from its traditional place in the Roman liturgy? And especially, why did the intentions disappear? One possible answer is this word from Gregory I (590-603): "At daily Mass we omit what is customarily said on these days and say only Kyrie eleison and Christe eleison." This abbreviation eventually became the common practice. By the end of the eighth century the number was fixed at three *Kyries*, three *Christes*, and three *Kyries*. This pattern gives the chant a trinitarian emphasis, but that interpretation is secondary; from ancient times, the East addressed this supplication to Christ.

The *Gloria in excelsis* followed the Kyrie, a hymn that dates back to the early church. Until the sixth century it was sung at morning prayer, then it was introduced into the Roman Mass on Christmas. Finally, its use was extended to Sundays and feasts of the martyrs at Masses when the bishop presides, and later on, in Frankish lands, to those same Masses, even when the presbyters presided in place of the bishops.

The Liturgy of the Word

A subdeacon proclaimed the first reading, which could be taken from any book of the Scriptures other than the Gospels or the Book of Psalms. The responsorial psalm followed. On occasion the singing of this psalm had been entrusted to a deacon, but Gregory the Great (590-604) abolished this practice when he saw that it led to abuses. Ministers had been chosen according to their singing ability. This psalm will later be called the "Gradual," since it is customarily sung from a "step" (*gradus*) of the ambo. The melody accompanying the text eventually became so ornate that only one verse of the psalm was ever sung.

The gospel was read with the greatest solemnity. During the *Alleluia*, the deacon appointed to proclaim the gospel approached the altar, picked up the book, and lifted it above his head. Two acolytes bearing candles, and three subdeacons, one carrying an incense pan or censer, walked with him to the ambo. A subdeacon indicated the appropriate passage, and the deacon marked the page with his finger. Then he ascended the ambo and proclaimed the word of God. After he had descended, a subdeacon received the gospel book in the folds of his chasuble, presented it to be kissed by all the ministers, then placed it in its case.

During Gregory's time, the bishop's homily was still an important moment in the celebration, but it fell into disuse as the Carolingian era approached. *Ordo I* did not even mention it.

The *Credo* did not appear in the Roman Mass until the eleventh century when it was introduced at the insistence of the Emperor Henry. It has been

> ### The Creed Is Introduced into Spain
>
> Out of respect for the holy faith and to strengthen weak spirits, the sacred council, with the agreement of our pious and very glorious lord, King Reccared, has decided that all the churches of Spain, Gaul, and Galatia, are to recite, as do the churches of the East, the symbol of faith of the Council of Constantinople, that is, of the 150 bishops. Thus, before the Lord's Prayer is said, it will be proclaimed aloud by the people, so that they openly witness the true faith and so that hearts are prepared for receiving with purified faith the body and blood of Christ.
>
> *Third Council of Toledo (589), Chapter 2*

recited in the Rhineland, however, since the time of Charlemagne. In Spain the creed was introduced at the end of the sixth century, at the time the Visigoths renounced Arianism. For that reason, its position is just before the "Our Father." Opposition to Arianism had also been the motive a number of years earlier, for introducing the creed in the eastern churches, where it is generally said between the presentation of the gifts and the beginning of the anaphora.

Preparation of the Gifts

All that remained of the general intercessory prayer was the presider's invitation to pray, the *Oremus*, which, as it were, ended suddenly since the offertory takes place immediately. This rather lengthy rite consisted in the pope's reception of the bread and wine brought by the faithful. Afterwards, the deacons covered the altar with a large cloth known as the "corporal."

The pope proceeded to the entrance of the sanctuary, on the men's side of the church. The members of the *senatorium*, that is, the noble Roman families, approached first. Each man gave the pope a small loaf of bread, which a subdeacon immediately placed on a cloth held between two acolytes. The archdeacon who always accompanied the pope received from each one a small flask of wine that was poured into a chalice held by a subdeacon. Once this chalice was filled, it was emptied into a larger receptacle carried by the acolytes. The pope and ministers then moved to the women's side of the church, and the same procedure was followed for these noble ladies. The other members of the faithful then came forward, but by now other ministers had replaced the pope and the archdeacon.

Those who had received the offerings then washed their hands, and the archdeacon placed the bread for the eucharist on the altar. The wine, in a cup with two handles, and the pope's offering of two loaves were also placed on the altar at this time. The schola, which had been singing a psalm during these entire processions, had not participated in this action; now it manifested its part by presenting the water to the subdeacon, who poured it into the chalice in the sign of the cross—undoubtedly this large gesture was intended to intermingle the wine and water. Much later it was interpreted as a blessing.

The pope concluded the offertory at the altar, as he said the prayer over the gifts.

Now began the anaphora or the canon of action, *Incipit canon actionis*, as it was called in an old Roman sacramentary. The wording of the canon has remained fixed since the time of Pope Gregory, although the texts of the Canon that come to us from this period do not contain the intercession for the dead. This intercession also appears to be of ancient composition, but perhaps its use was limited to Masses celebrated for the deceased.

The Conclusion of the Canon

When the bishop says *Per ipsum et cum ipso*, the archdeacon lifts the chalice, holding it by the handles with the [linen called] *offertorium*, and holds it on high, next to the bishop.

The bishop touches the side of the chalice with the breads while saying *Per ipsum et cum ipso* up to the *Per omnia saecula saeculorum*. Then he places the breads in their place, and the archdeacon, having removed the *offertorium* from the chalice's handles, places the chalice next to the bread.

Ordo I, nn. 89-90

The "Our Father" before the Breaking of the Bread

Someone coming from Italy informed me that some of his friends—I don't know whether they are Latins or Greeks—murmur against my decisions, under the pretext of promoting the holy Roman Church. "How," they say, "can we resist the influence of the churches of Constantinople if we follow their customs in all things?" I asked him what were these customs that we imitate. He answered that we have decided to . . . say the *Kyrie eleison* and the Lord's Prayer immediately after the Canon. But my response to him was that we have not, on any of these points, attempted to follow the customs of another church.

This is why we say the Lord's Prayer immediately after the [eucharistic] prayer: the custom of the apostles was to consecrate the offering only through the prayer of oblation. It seemed to me that it was not at all fitting to say over the offering a prayer composed by any writer whatsoever and not to say over the body and blood of the Redeemer the prayer he himself composed, a prayer handed down to us by tradition. Even though among the Greeks this prayer is said by all the people, among us the priest alone says it.

Gregory I: Letter 12 to John of Syracuse (598)

The eucharistic prayer was interrupted solely for the singing of the *Sanctus*, and even the presider made only one gesture during this prayer. At its conclusion he took the two breads he himself had presented and touches the cup held aloft by the deacon. By so doing, he recalled that the offering of the Son must be returned to the Father; Jesus' offering became, then, the church's offering through this act in the Holy Spirit.

The "Our Father," the Kiss of Peace, and the Breaking of the Bread

Pope Gregory inverted the order of the fraction and the saying of the Our Father. Some believed that he did so to imitate Constantinople, but his motive, he said, was to give this prayer a rank approaching that of the consecratory formula. The fact that in the Roman tradition the priest alone sang this prayer emphasizes this function. The last request was extended in the embolism, or expansion, that followed: "Deliver us, Lord, from all evil . . . give us peace in our time . . ."

This phrase led directly to the rite introduced by the presider's words: "May the peace of the Lord be always with you." The archdeacon, according to *Ordo I*, extended the peace to the first bishop, "and then the others [gave it] in order, and then the people."

The breaking of the bread, the fraction, took on significant length: the acolytes received the consecrated breads in small linen sacks. Then they approached the bishops and priests who broke the breads into as many pieces as necessary for the communion. Meanwhile, the schola sang the *Agnus Dei*. This litany was introduced by Pope Sergius I at the end of the seventh century. The symbolism of the broken body of the immolated Lamb of the new passover was joined to the sign of the father dividing the food for his family, a customary practice at Jewish meals.

The Communion

The history of this period suggests that many of the Roman faithful desired to be nourished by the eucharist, although this practice had already eroded in numerous churches. In Milan, even during the time of Ambrose, the Greeks received the eucharist only once a year, and, in Gaul, the bishop solemnly blessed the people before the body and blood of Christ were distributed. Regardless of explanations given for this blessing, the reason is that the assembly was dismissed immediately afterwards, with only a small number of people remaining in church to share at the Lord's table.

According to *Ordo I*, the pope at his chair received the paten and another chalice into which he placed the remains of the bread from which he had communicated. The archdeacon announced the day and place for the next "station." Then the other bishops and priests received the eucharist. The procession that formed immediately afterwards resembled that at the offertory: the faithful, beginning with the nobility, came forward and received a portion of the consecrated bread. Then they were "confirmed" by a deacon; that is, they drank from a cup presented to them by a minister. These cups, although containing wine, had not been placed on the altar for the eucharistic prayer. Instead, a small amount of the consecrated wine from the pope's chalice was poured into them at this time.

Meanwhile, the schola sang a psalm, which they concluded (at a sign from the bishop) with the *Gloria Patri*.

The Concluding Rite

The presider, standing at the altar, said the concluding prayer (*oratio ad complendum*). Then, after he had greeted the people, the deacon dismissed them: *Ite, missa est*. The acolytes with the seven candles and the subdeacon with the censer preceded the presider as they recessed. When the pope passed in front of the bishops, they requested his blessing. He blessed them with the words: "May the Lord bless you," and repeated this blessing over the priests and people he met on his way to the sacristy.

The Mass in the Other Rites

The Roman tendency that we have just explored, namely the tendency to clothe the rites with more solemn forms, is a universal phenomenon.

Among the Greeks, the litanies and other supplications began to multiply at this time: the deacon came and went between sanctuary and nave to help people unite themselves to the priest's prayer. Often enough the prayer was silent, even during the anaphora. When the presider raised his voice, the people responded by means of acclamations, like the "Amen" after the words of Christ during the institution narrative. This narrative, however, was considered less important than the epiclesis. We have already noted how the rites introducing the liturgy of the word and the liturgy of the eucharist were given prominence: the "Little Entrance" with the gospel procession, and the "Great Entrance" with the solemn procession of the gifts.

No doubt it was during this period that intinction was introduced, namely the practice of dipping the eucharistic bread into the chalice before the bread was given to the people. On the other hand, the incense burner was no longer hand-held; rather, balanced and suspended from chains, it spread perfume about the altar, before the icons, and throughout the whole church.

The practice of adding solemnity to the rites also spread throughout the West: the Ambrosian liturgy at Milan and the liturgies of Gaul and Spain enriched their own traditions by borrowing from the East.

Surviving documents give us some idea of the Gallican Mass in the seventh century. The entrance rites were composed of the *Aius* ("Holy God, Strong One . . .") sung in Greek and in Latin, and the biblical canticle of Zachary, followed by the "collect after the prophecy." The liturgy of the Word had three readings, preceded on feasts of martyrs by an account of the martyr's passion. The first reading was followed by a psalm, the second by the canticle of the three children in the furnace; the gospel was framed by the repetition of the *Aius*. The general prayer, litanic in form, concluded with the "collect after the prayer."

The eucharistic liturgy began with a long monition that explained the meaning of the particular feast. Then the deacon brought the bread and the

---

Extracts from a Gallican Mass at Christmas

Collect after the names — Lord Jesus, we ask you to receive favorably this sacrifice of praise which today is offered and which we offer to you in honor of your incarnation; to those who remain here below, give life; to the deceased, give eternal rest; write in eternity the names of those read aloud, since it is for them that you revealed yourself in the flesh. You are the savior of the world. Together with the Father who is coeternal with you, you live and reign.

Collect after the peace — Eternal and all-powerful God, you consecrated this day of your incarnation, this day when the Blessed Virgin Mary gave birth. Through the mystery of the incarnation you became the cornerstone; you brought together the angels and all those separated by ancient discord and by transgressions connected with the ancient tree. In the joy of this feast give your family the happiness of being close to you in the same flesh and of being made one with the citizens of heaven from whom you took the body you assumed. May the bodily kiss which unites them bring about the disappearance of discords, which divide those who have the joy of seing you. Being their creator, you have become one in nature with them in the flesh. Grant this . . .

Missale gothicum

In Gaul the People Are Blessed before Communion

Through Moses the Lord confided to the priesthood the task of blessing the people: "Speak to Aaron and his sons and tell them: 'This is how you shall bless the people: the Lord bless you and keep you'" (Nm 6:22-27). Aaron represents the bishop and his sons represent the priests. To both the Lord has given the mission of blessing the people; but to emphasize the honor reserved to the holy pontiff, the laws of the church prescribe that the bishop pronounce a longer blessing, whereas the priests say a shorter one: "May the faith, charity, and the sharing of the body and blood of our Lord Jesus Christ be always with you." It is permitted to bless in this way because the Lord established it, and no one can contradict the priests because "Heaven and earth will pass away, but my words will not pass away." This is why the blessing is given before the communion, so that the sacrament of the blessing be placed in a vessel that has been blessed.

Pseudo-Germanus (8th century),
Expositio antiquae missae gallicanae, 1. 24

wine to the altar in vessels made in the form of a tower, recalling Christ's tomb in Jerusalem. The names of those making the offering were then read; and the peace was shared. The first of these rites was followed by the "collect after the names"; the second, by the "collect after the peace." The wording of the anaphora was variable, with only the *Pridie* or institution narrative having a fixed form. The surviving books also contain proper prayers for each Mass: the *Immolatio* which corresponded to the preface; the *Post Sanctus*; and the *Post pridie* or *Post mysteria*.

Immediately before the "Our Father" the bread was broken. The bishop pronounced a solemn blessing to close the celebration for those who did not communicate. Only those who will receive the eucharist remained in church after this blessing. And they were probably a minority.

Concelebration

The catechetical instructions written at Jerusalem about the year 400 indicate (concerning the rite of concelebration) that the deacon washed the hands of the bishop and priests who stood around the altar. Pseudo-Dionysius (ca. 500) mentioned the same rite and its meaning: "Those who will proceed to the sacred action must be purified." Thus it was not necessary to pronounce the text to be considered an actor in the holy Mysteries.

At the Council of Constantinople (680) a Latin bishop, Fortunius of Carthage, celebrated with the Greeks although he certainly did not know Greek well enough to read the eucharistic prayer. The only question asked before he was to "celebrate the liturgy" was whether he should be placed before or after the metropolitan bishops who were present. We find an analogous situation in Pope John VIII's letter responding to a complaint of Photius: the two Roman priests who were sent as legates did not wish to celebrate with the patriarch (the Latin text here reads "to consecrate with you").

At Rome this form of concelebration was considered legitimate, since the refusal of the pope's representatives was not based on any incompatibility of rites. Nevertheless, a different practice was gaining currency. *Ordo III*, which seems to have appeared in the eighth century, contained precise details for the ceremonial of the stational Mass on major feasts of the year: the cardinal priests who surround their bishop at the altar were to say the Canon with him. Since each cardinal priest holds a corporal with three eucharistic breads, they cannot make any gesture, but they unite themselves to the presider by saying the prayer. *Ordo III* was presented as a codicil to *Ordo I* and was almost contemporaneous with it. *Ordo I*, however, specified that only the pope stands erect after the *Sanctus*; the other bishops and priests continue to bow. This practice would seem to exclude any vocal participation in the prayer. Was the practice of vocal concelebration introduced during the interval between the composition of each of these documents, or was it more ancient? All we can say is that vocal concelebration was not primitive.

* * * *

Clearly in this development of the missarum sollemnia, the liturgy has lost something of its primitive simplicity. As members of the pontifical court assumed greater prominence, so did the specialists in chant. They adopted more ornate melodies, which effectively reduced the assembly's participation. The strength of the Mass during these years is that the bishop always appeared as the one presiding at prayer, just as he was known to preside over the whole life of the people. The evolution ahead will, unfortunately, weaken this characteristic of the Mass as a common "action," an action that vividly mirrors the image of the church.

Further Reading

Joseph Jungmann, *The Mass of the Roman Rite* (1 volume edition) 50-56.
Theodor Klauser, *A Short History of the Roman Liturgy* 59-72.
Herman Wegman, *Christian Worship in East and West* 183-185.

Chapter V

The "Celebrant"
VIII - XII century

The Roman Mass in France and Spain

Well before the Carolingian period, the liturgy of Rome had become the liturgy of all Italy, except in northern regions that remained faithful to the rite of Milan. It had also become the liturgy of the missionary churches in England and Germany. But a vast territory, extending from Ireland to Spain, had escaped its influence.

In Gaul, meanwhile, and as early as the seventh century, private initiatives had been undertaken to import Roman books and combine their texts with local usages. The latter really needed a breath of fresh air: the lack of copyists and clerical ignorance had allowed the old manuscripts to fall into ruin. Further, the region had no ecclesiastical authority to convoke councils, which had earlier—at the time of Caesarius of Arles (470-542)—

The Franks Discover Roman Chant

Nearly all of France desired to acquire a deeper knowledge of the manner of singing [of the Romans]. When Pope Stephen went to France to see Pepin, the father of the emperor Charlemagne, in order to defend the rights of the Holy See which were being menaced by the Lombards, it was Stephen, through his clergy and with the assistance of the king, who introduced this usage into this country, a usage which has widely spread elsewhere.

Walafrid Strabo, Liber de exordiis et incrementis, 26

---

helped shape the Gallican tradition. The princes of the new ruling family often took matters into their own hands; but Pepin the Short (714-768), undoubtedly impressed by the splendor of the papal liturgy celebrated by Pope Stephen II at his (Pepin's) coronation in the Abbey of St. Denis, backed away from the difficulties involved in restoring the indigenous rites. His solution was to use the books coming from Italy as the basis for a reformed Frankish sacramentary. Today this book is known as the "Gelasian sacramentary of the eighth century"; it was constantly recopied and used for a number of years. In addition, Pepin sanctioned the adoption of the Roman chant, assisted in this endeavor by two bishops, Chrodegang of Metz and Remedius of Rouen.

Charlemagne (ca. 742-814) envisioned an even more radical solution: he decided to put together and impose one missal on the whole empire. Thus he obtained from Pope Hadrian I a copy of the Gregorian Sacramentary. But since this book was intended to be used for the papal liturgy, it was incapable of responding to all the needs of the local Frankish community. Benedict of Aniane, a monk from the south of France, prepared a supplement to the missal that incorporated Roman texts already known in the country and also a small number of local customs that no one wanted to abandon. Additional liturgical books had to be imported from Rome, since the Franks soon realized that besides the texts of the prayers to be said, they also needed to include in their ceremonials descriptions of how the rites were to be celebrated, so the Roman *Ordines*, too, were recopied and adapted.

Such a transformation does not take place overnight: some priests remained attached to the traditional liturgy, and certain members of the faithful were bewildered by all the changes. Further, the required books were difficult to obtain; their exemplars were rare and required much time to copy. It is not surprising, therefore, that clerics continued to use whatever manuscripts were available to them. The practical need was so pressing, however, and Charlemagne's order so authoritative that with surprising speed the "new liturgy" eventually triumphed over all alternative practices.

During the tenth century the liturgy of Rome, in its turn, fell into deep decadence. Its renaissance had now to come from the north which, having conserved the treasures of the Roman liturgy, would return them— seasoned to French taste—to the church from which they had come.

The ancient Hispanic-Gallican tradition still exists in Europe—south of the Pyrenees, except in the Catalonian dioceses attached to the ecclesiastical province of Narbonne. At the end of the eleventh century Gregory VII

Charlemagne on Roman Unity

Just as Peter held first place among the apostles and their disciples, so it is immediately recognized that the Roman See holds first place among all sees established by the apostles or their disciples . . . Although from the earliest ages of the faith, our church has remained united to the Roman See in holy religion, it has somewhat distanced itself in the celebration of the liturgy, and yet this is not opposed to the faith. But when Stephen, the venerable and holy bishop of Rome, visited Gaul, it was through the zeal and solicitude of King Pepin, our very illustrious and noble father of happy memory, that our church came to be linked to that of Rome as regards the arrangement of the psalmody so that, just as there is but one zeal in belief, so there is but one way of singing. Churches united by the holy reading of the one holy law should also be united by the venerable practice of a unified modulation of voices; differences in celebration must not separate those who religiously adhere to one faith.

This is what we ourselves have done, after receiving from God the kingdom of Italy, and desiring to heighten the dignity of the holy Roman Church and obeying the beneficial exhortations of the very reverend Pope Hadrian: many churches of this country which formerly refused the tradition of the Holy See in psalmody are now eagerly embracing it, and united to the Roman Church by their faith, they are also united to it by their manner of singing.

We see this not only in all the provinces of Gaul, in Germany and in Italy, but also among the Saxons and those people of the north, called by God through us, who have recently converted to the true faith.

Livres carolins I.1, ch. 6

Pope Hadrian I Writes to Charlemagne

As to the sacramentary arranged by our predecessor Pope Gregory, you have asked us through the grammarian Paul for an authentic copy that conforms to the tradition of our holy church; we have sent this to your royal excellency by the monk John, abbot from the city of Ravenna.

Letter 69

(1073-1085) enforced Roman discipline on the whole peninsula, doing so with the assistance of the strict Cluniac abbeys (benedictine reformed) of which he was a product. As Spain was reconquered for Christianity, this reform was progressively imposed on the whole country. But at Toledo resistance remained so strong that the old rite continued to exist in some churches. It was reorganized in the sixteenth century and reformed after Vatican II.

"The Priest Alone Enters into the Prayer"

The Roman Mass in the seventh century was still the action of the people. When the presider intervened, he always spoke in a loud voice so that everyone could hear him. And when he addressed God in the intercessions, the benefits he sought concerned the sanctification of all the faithful. The presider stayed in the background, as it were, behind his mission of serving the church at prayer. Such service was a characteristic of all the ancient liturgies.

About the ninth century a different image of the presider appeared in the West, although it seems to have been more ancient in the East: the image of the Jewish high priest who alone enters the holy of holies. This image progressively changed the way ministers were seen. The powers received by the bishop or priest accorded him such a privileged status, compared to other Christians, that the essential liturgical action seems to belong to him alone. Therefore, the priests began at this time to say silently the texts that they had formerly proclaimed aloud, beginning with the most important: the canon, or anaphora. The manuscripts from this period contain the following notice after the *Sanctus*: "The bishop alone enters into the Canon, and says it in a low voice." As a result, the eucharistic prayer was considered to begin only at this moment. The prayer now known as the preface continued to be sung or read aloud. In the manuscripts, its variable character was set off from the unchangeable section of the Canon by means of illuminations, in the form of a cross and at times filling a whole page, on the first letter of the *Te igitur*.

The same phenomenon extended to other prayers, like the prayer over the gifts; in time it came to be known as the "secret."

Praying toward the East
and Celebrating with "One's Back to the People"

The custom of orienting oneself in prayer (facing toward a specific direction) is found in many religions, but its appearance in Christianity had some unique features. First, for Christians orientation in prayer is not a requirement as it is in other forms of worship, since the New Testament calls us to go beyond such details. When such orientation was adopted, it was not geographic: the Jew turning toward Jerusalem or the Moslem turning toward Mecca faces east or west, depending on whether one is in Algeria or in Pakistan. The Christian, on the other hand, turns to God by facing the direction from which the sun rises, no matter where one is.

Witnesses to this practice abound in the east from the earliest centuries, and we do not include those churches whose apse is in the east and where the altar is close to the apse or even attached to the rear wall; here the priest says the eucharistic prayer with his back to the assembly. Similar concerns and architectural situations required an adaptation of the Roman liturgy when it entered Gaul during the Carolingian period. Because in Rome most basilicas faced the west, the presider faced the people and prayed facing the direction in which the sun rises. The books imported from Rome and edited for use by the Franks show signs of adjustment. No reason other than the orientation of religious buildings led the eucharistic presider to stand in front of rather than behind the altar. This change, however, so agreed with the direction popular understanding was taking that it encountered almost no resistance. The assembly simply had no difficulty accepting their isolation from the sacred minister as he entered before them into the holy mysteries.

The Private Prayers of the Priest and Ministers

The Roman liturgy, once introduced into Frankish lands, was embellished with prayers said silently or semiprivately among the ministers. These prayers consisted in large part of "apologies," namely, formulas declaring the unworthiness of the sinner called to such a ministry. Their purpose was to purify the minister but the confessions did not always avoid an excess of complacent self-accusation. Some prayers accompanied actions that formerly were done in silence, such as uncovering the chalice, placing incense in the censer, using the censer, the washing of hands, and others. These actions provided occasions for brief ejaculatory prayers, and helped fulfill the tendency to wrap even the most unimportant gestures in the sacred.

These silent and semiprivate prayers occurred throughout the celebration, but they increased at moments that easily lend themselves to privacy: the entrance rites when the ministers arrive in the sanctuary, the preparation of the gifts at the beginning of the Holy Mysteries, before communion as the faithful prepare to share at the holy table. These formulas were taken from the most diverse sources—from old Roman or Gallican sacramentaries

An Example of the Priest's Private Prayer

Before going to the altar. O Lord, I am unworthy of your sanctuary, and each day I harm myself through innumerable sins. Do I have the audacity to address you with amicable prayers, and yet very often offend you by my evil actions? You have me take medicines because I am sick; for my part, I do everything to compromise my health. I read your law contained in the holy books but, unhappy as I am, I neglect this salutary teaching. I approach your altar as if I were faithful, and yet with a hardened heart I separate myself from your commandments. O Lord, give me a heart that can be touched so that I will truly hate sin. If you grant me the grace, I will weep for my sins; you, in return, will make my sins like snow. And even though I have lost the palm [of victory], even though I am deceived by the enemy, let me at least obtain pardon through your mercy. To you, O God, king of all kingdoms, is the honor of ruling the universe for ages and ages.

While going up to the altar. O Lord, in the presence of your divine majesty I confess my sins to the saints who are here [allusion to the relics placed within the altar] and to you, my God and my creator: I have sinned by pride, hatred, cupidity, avarice, fornication, and impurity, intemperance and drunkenness, and by all the vices that flow from them. And what now? I have separated myself by seeing, smelling, tasting, and touching, in a word, in thought, word, and deed. Just as you justify the impious, may you also justify me, and make me rise [pass] from death to life, O Lord, my God.

While placing the bread and wine upon the altar. O all powerful God, I ask you to receive this offering. Wipe away the sins of those who offer it and of those for whom it is offered. O Lord, may we, with a humble spirit and a contrite heart, be received by you.

Sacramentary of Amiens (2nd half of the 9th century)

66

(where they do not appear as private prayers) to books of personal devotion which, beginning with the Carolingian period, were widespread among certain levels of society. The introduction of these texts into the liturgy was done locally and did not take place in the same manner everywhere; in fact, we often find the same texts in different regions and with some variations. The way they were grouped together, however, allowed for a multitude of different combinations, and gave the impression of great diversity.

The priest was also invited to prepare privately for Mass by reciting prayers that did not form part of the liturgy proper but which, beginning in the eleventh century, were introduced into the sacramentaries as psalms, verses, and orations. Similar prayers were to be recited after the celebration. The number of these texts increased in the thirteenth century. Other formulas were recorded as prayers accompanying the vesting of the presider; these texts proposed allegorical interpretations for each vestment of the priest or bishop. The variety of such texts during and after the Carolingian period was endless. Many of these prayers eventually found their way into the Missal of Pius V.

Private Masses

Evidence of how the "celebrant's" role was exalted in the Latin Churches is found in a practice still unknown in the East today, except among Catholics: the private Mass. By private Mass we do not mean a eucharist celebrated with a small group, even if the celebration is in someone's home, since the people in the latter sitution are part of the Christian community (for example, Mass may be said with or for a family, an invalid, a confraternity). Such "home" liturgies take place with people and are celebrated on their behalf; the priest is called to preside over these small assemblies. The private Mass, on the other hand, is a Mass that is celebrated at the sole initiative of the priest. Such a Mass is private even if he offers the holy sacrifice for an intention requested by another. Normally at least a server who gives the responses is required.

These private celebrations increased from the Carolingian period onward, simultaneously with a growth in devotion to Masses for the deceased. All churches, both monastic and parochial, henceforth contained many altars.

Plenary Missals

The arrangement of the liturgical books was hardly convenient for priests celebrating privately. For each Mass numerous books were required: the sacramentary for the orations and eucharistic prayer; the

A Monk Prepares for a Private Mass

The priest who will celebrate Mass should first wash his hands in the church with the vessel prepared for this purpose. He places the host on the paten . . . then he takes the chalice in his right hand, in his left the cruets. His companion carries the priest's vestments, with the cincture on top, with the missal and the candle, and in this manner they proceed to the holy altar. As soon as the cruets are put in their proper place, the priest, on the right, and his companion, on the left, unfold the altar cloth. He places the chalice he has been holding in the middle of the altar; the missal is placed on the right side of the altar. Taking off his tunic, the priest bows before the altar. Meanwhile his companion unfolds the vestments, placing the alb over the priest's head while spreading apart its opening; he also gives the priest the cincture and maniple. Then the priest takes the stole and says *Confiteor Deo*; his companion responds *Misereatur vestri* and while the companion is saying the *Confiteor* the priest puts on the stole while kissing it and adds: *Indulgentiam et remissionem omnium peccatorum vestrorum* with the *Adiutorium nostrum in nomine Domini*. The priest then puts on the chasuble which his companion has carefully unfolded for him on his arms, smoothing out the amice underneath. Then having washed and dried his fingers, the priest bows and says a short prayer. After this he kisses the altar . . .

Constitutions of Cluny, redacted by Bernard (1068)

Sunday Celebrations and Private Masses

Masses said for particular intentions by priests on Sunday are not to be said in a public place, to avoid having people use this as an excuse for dispensing themselves from the communal celebration of Mass which takes place at the third hour, according to the canons. For this inaugurates a very bad habit among certain people who on Sundays and feasts vanish as soon as they have heard one Mass, even if it is for the deceased, so as to spend the whole day, from its earliest hours, in drinking or in debauchery rather than in serving God.

Theodulph, bishop of Orleans (789-818),

lectionary for the readings; the antiphonary for the chants though they were, in fact, usually read by the priest. Why not come up with something easier to handle, something more suitable? At first the various books were simply collected into one volume one after another. But it isn't long before the scriptural readings and the antiphons are incorporated into the sacramentary itself, either as marginal notes or with the text appearing at its appropriate place in the rite. This book was known as the complete missal, the "plenary missal"; it became popular about the year 1200.

The Eucharistic Bread and the Rites of Communion

In the eleventh century the use of unleavened bread, already found among the Armenians, became quite general in the West—leading us to conjecture that it must have been introduced a little before this date in some places. By this time, the faithful received the eucharist only rarely, and the presentation of the gifts had lost much of its meaning. Practical reasons, especially difficulties in preserving the sacred species under the form of leavened bread, undoubtedly played a role here as did the Gospel (the Last Supper occurred during the week of the unleavened bread). From this period, Latin theologians condemned the use of leavened bread, and eventually this practice became a topic of discussion with the eastern churches.

Also at this time the custom arose of receiving the eucharist on the tongue rather than in the hand. This innovation was considered a sign of respect and also led the assembly to kneel for convenience' sake while receiving the eucharist. The habit of kneeling was imposed only gradually, however, since contrary practices can be found even at the end of the Middle Ages.

The imposition of the Greek practice of receiving the eucharist by dipping the consecrated bread into the chalice did not succeed in the West. It was reprobated in 675 by the Council of Braga, and this council's text was often repeated in the eleventh century, notably by the Synod of Clermont in 1095. Reluctance in this regard, together with theological considerations, led in the thirteenth century to the practice of giving only the eucharistic bread to the laity.

The missals from this period no longer mention the communion of the faithful because on most occasions only the priest received the sacrament. When thirteenth-century theologians and mystical writers attempted to react against this abuse, they had to borrow other rites to respond to this new requirement. The rite for the sick was used: the *Confiteor* (I confess), the *Ecce Agnus Dei* (Behold the Lamb of God), and the triple *Domine, non sum dignus* (Lord, I am not worthy) based on the Centurion's prayer in Luke 7:6-7. At this point, communion was no longer seen as an intrinsic element in the Mass; communion bread previously consecrated and reserved was used for communion.

Unleavened Bread Is Legitimate

A letter addressed in your name to the people of Apulia manifests such great presumption on your part: with violence it attempts to prove that the Lord gave leavened bread to his disciples at the Last Supper as the sacrament of his body. This is totally false, as can easily be seen from the two Testaments. In fact, Christ did not come to abolish the Law, but to fulfill the ancient Passover according to the precept of this Law, with unleavened bread and wine. It is thus that he, with unleavened bread and wine, has handed on the new [Passover] to his disciples, as Luke clearly states.

Leo IX, Letter to Michael Cerularius,
Patriarch of Constantinople (1053-1054)

Communion No Longer Given in the Hand

The eucharist is not to be placed in the hands of any of the laity, or of any woman, but only in the mouth and with the words: "May the body and blood of the Lord profit for the remission of sins and for eternal life." Should anyone transgress this, he is to be removed from the altar; to do the opposite is to despise the all-powerful God and, insofar as it be possible, to show God a lack of respect.

Regino of Prüm (d. 915), De synodalibus causis
et disciplinis ecclesiasticis I, 202

"Do not dip the bread into the chalice"

Let no one communicate from the altar except by receiving the bread and the wine separately, except in case of necessity and with taking all precaution.

Council of Clermont (presided over by
Pope Urban II, 1095)

The Prayer of the People

All these changes conspired to enhance the importance of the priest. Once the presbyter performs actions that were originally distributed among many ministers, he becomes the "celebrant." The same dynamic reduces the people's role, when they are present at all, to the passive attitude of spectators. The idea that one "presides" over a liturgical action and even the idea of a gathering—an assembly—lose their footing; the terms became increasingly rare and finally disappeared altogether. The understanding of the eucharist as joined to a gathering of the faithful was lost; so was the notion of the assembly as a local manifestation of the universal church.

On the contrary, concern for one's individual salvation assumed a larger role in popular piety. Christians and their pastors were of one mind: the holy sacrifice was a means for acquiring divine help; and each person sought to apply this help to him- or herself. People desired that the Mass help the deceased; they believed that grace increased in proportion to the number of Masses celebrated. Therefore, "foundations" were established: the generosity of princes and nobles ensured that Masses would be celebrated for their intentions and for the success of their undertakings. One's liturgical participation was no longer necessary, since the community was thought to be present in the priest accomplishing his ministry.

The people no longer had access to the heart of the celebration; the essential prayers were said in a low voice and in Latin, which was no longer the language they understood and spoke. As a result, they were compelled to seek spiritual nourishment in marginal and peripheral elements. Imagination clothed the rites with edifying and moralizing meanings, even those rites that were originally simply practical. These "allegorical" interpretations are found in small treatises called *Expositiones Missae* or Explanations of the Mass. Bishop Amalarius of Metz (775-832) was one of the originators of this literary genre. Consider also the popular developments in liturgical singing: superimposed on the Latin or vernacular texts are embellishments—melismatic vocalizing—sung by the cantors; these pieces are called "tropes." Such compositions, especially the *Alleluias*, led to new compositions with verses in meter, and with texts that either rhyme or use words with similar vowel sounds. These sequels, or "sequences," occurring in the midst of the liturgy of the word, only divert people's attention from the proper function of this moment in the celebration.

Finally, rules adopted for the private Mass contaminated other forms of celebration. Eventually the priest became the "celebrant" who alone says Mass, even parts that should have been sung or read by other ministers.

An Allegorical Commentary:
The Proclamation of the Gospel at Mass

The deacon goes to the altar where he picks up the gospel book from which he will read. The altar can stand for Jerusalem since, according to the Scriptures, the proclamation of the Gospel comes from this city: "For from Zion will come the Law, and from Jerusalem the word of the Lord" (Is 2:3). The altar can also stand for the body of the Lord himself, in whom are the words of the Gospel, namely, the Good News. It is Christ who ordered the apostles to preach the Gospel to every creature; it is Christ who said: "my words are spirit and life" (Is 6:64). His words are contained in the Gospel. The deacon who carries the book is, as it were, the feet of Christ. He carries the book upon his right shoulder; this evokes the life of this world in which the Gospel must be announced.

When the deacon greets the people, it is fitting that all turn toward him. The priest and the people are in fact facing the East till the moment when the Lord speaks through the deacon, and they sign themselves on their foreheads . . . And why on this particular part of the body? The reason is that the forehead is the seat of shame. If the Jews were ashamed to believe in the one whom they desired to crucify, as the Apostle says—"We proclaim Christ crucified, a stumbling block to the Jews" (1 Cor 1:23)—we believe that we are saved by the Crucified One. The Jews were ashamed of his name, whereas we believe that this name protects us. This is why we make the sign of the cross on the forehead, which is the seat of shame, as we have said.

. . . The two candles carried before the gospel book stand for the Law and the Prophets which preceded the gospel teaching. The censer evokes all the virtues that flow from the life of Christ. The censer-bearer ascends the ambo before the gospel so as to spread the odor of perfume, thus showing that Christ did good before announcing the Gospel, as Luke in the Acts of the Apostles attests: "All that Jesus did and taught" (Acts 1:1). He first acted and then taught.

The elevated place from which the Gospel is read shows the superiority of the teaching of the Gospel and its great authority of judgment. The location of the candles shows that the Law and the Prophets are inferior to the Gospel. And when the book, after the reading, is returned to its place, the candles are extinguished since it is the preaching of the

>>>>

Gospel that continues, the Law and the Prophets speaking no longer . . .

The rites before the gospel stand for Christ's preaching up to the hour of his passion as well as that of those who preach to the end of the world and beyond. The rites after the gospel reveal what has been brought about by Christ's passion, resurrection, and ascension into heaven, and likewise the sacrifice, mortification, and resurrection of his disciples who profess the faith . . .

Amalarius of Metz, Liber officialis, III, ch. 18.

* * * *

We can truly speak of these centuries as a spiritual turning point and cultural mutation. New forms of celebration had greatly influenced the way the Latin world prayed. The Roman liturgy was no longer linked to the culture of a Mediterranean people and no longer joined to values received from the past. The whole western world followed essentially the same rites—those inherited from the tradition of Rome, the eternal city, the Apostolic See. A certain flexibility appeared, however, at the entrance rites, the offertory, the communion, and the concluding rites. The private prayers of the priest and his ministers differed in detail, yet they hardly involved the faithful. The eucharistic prayer, now said silently, no longer appeared to concern the people and the sung parts of the liturgy are rendered by specialists who leave only small portions to the nonchoir members of the assembly.

Further Reading

Cheslyn Jones and others, eds., *The Study of Liturgy* 220-240.

Joseph Jungmann, *The Mass of the Roman Rite* (1 volume edition) 56-70.

Theodor Klauser, *A Short History of the Western Liturgy* 77-84.

H.A. Reinhold, "Liturgy, Allegorical Interpretations of," *New Catholic Encyclopedia*, vol. 8, 937-938.

Herman Wegman, *Christian Worship in East and West* 143-149.

James F. White, "Traditions, Liturgical, in the West: Pre-Reformation," in *The New Dictionary of Sacramental Worship*, ed. Peter E. Fink. Collegeville: The Liturgical Press, 1272-1282.

Chapter VI

Seeing and Adoring the Host
XII - XV century

The evolutions that began in the Carolingian period continued to the end of the Middle Ages. Toward the end of the twelfth century, however, a renewal of parish life—with the ringing of church bells and the solemn celebration of feast days—stands as a beacon in the midst of darkness. In the following century the preaching of the new mendicant orders--the Franciscans, Dominicans, and Carmelites—will promote the growth of religious sentiment and morality. Theological reflection will flourish and accompany these transformations affecting sacramental practice. Yet in spite of this renewal, the people's participation in the Mass will be minimal; they will remain at the fringe of the eucharistic action.

Rood-Screens, Pulpits, and Choir

In cathedrals and in the monastic churches, the laity find themselves behind a veritable wall of wood or stone which concealed from view the actions now performed by the specialists of the celebration. This enclosure is incorrectly compared to the eastern iconostasis. The iconostasis encloses only the altar and its immediate surroundings; the readers and the schola remain close to the faithful, and the deacons come and go through the doors of communication. In the West, on the other hand, everything took place behind the "rood-screen." The people were not only separated from the sanctuary but also from the "choir," that is, from those who were allowed to participate in the sacred action. The faithful become mute; they "hear Mass," to use the expression that was henceforth popular. Even in parishes having no rood-screen, clerics of lesser rank who had been instructed in sacred singing and who served the offices stood close to the celebrant and responded to his prayers. They were located in front of the faithful, who having been reduced to spectators and left to themselves, took recourse in all kinds of pious devotions.

Preaching itself, though revitalized by the mendicant orders was detached from the liturgy. No longer did one preach at the chair or at the ambo, both once located near the altar. Instead, the preacher ascended a high pulpit in the nave and preached a homily no longer based on the readings that had been proclaimed. Instead, the homily became a dogmatic and moral exposition that at times gave way to rhetoric and admonitions that could just as easily have taken place outside Mass.

The Rite of the Elevation

The only moment in the celebration that still attracted the interest of the faithful was the consecration. Reactions to the errors of Berengarius, the eleventh-century monk who had disparaged faith in the Lord's real presence in the eucharistic species, drew attention to the words of Christ: "This is my body . . . This is my blood." These words, in turn, became isolated from the eucharistic prayer. Since they were said quietly, priests usually accompanied these words with gestures in order to call attention to them. On the other hand, people who rarely received the eucharist, did at least want to see the host. The priest, who held the bread in his hands for the institution account, thus began to elevate it high enough for the people to see. In order to avoid abuses, a synodal decree from Paris (ca. 1200), instructed the priest not to elevate the host till after the words of consecration are pronounced. The "elevation" spread rapidly throughout much of the West; the last quarter of the thirteenth century witnessed the elevation of the chalice as well.

In some places, to emphasize the importance of the elevation, a bell was rung; elsewhere a candle was lit at morning Masses while the church still remained in darkness; at times a dark curtain, drawn by a machine, rose up behind the altar in order to make the elevated host stand out clearly. This viewing worked best, of course, when the host looked less like bread— when it was white, round, without thickness, having something of the immaterial about it, and when it presented no obstacle to the desire to contemplate a transcendent presence having nothing to do with the banal realities of daily life.

The Elevation

Priests as they begin the words *Qui pridie* of the Canon of the Mass are forbidden to raise the host they hold high enough to be seen by the people; they are to hold it about level with their chest till they have said the *Hoc est corpus meum*; and then they elevate the host so that everyone can see it.

Synodal Statutes of Paris (beginning of the 13th century)

A Bishop's Directives on the Elevation

The host should be raised high enough so that it can be seen by all present. In this way the people's devotion to the host will increase, as well as the quality of their faith. Parishioners should be exhorted not to be content with bowing since this shows too little respect at the moment when Christ is elevated; rather, they are to kneel and adore their Creator with devotion and respect. A little bell will be rung beforehand as an invitation to kneel; at the elevation a large bell will be rung three times.

Guvil, Bishop of Exeter, Decree of 1287

Rewards in Heaven

Gertrude received this light; a person's merits for heaven will increase in proportion to the number of times this person looks with love and desire at the holy host containing the sacramental body of Christ. In fact, the special delicacies a person will taste in heaven will correspond to the number of times this person, while on earth, looked at or at least desired to do so, the body of Christ.

Revelations of St. Gertrude of Hefta (1256-1301), IV, ch. 25.

✣

St. Dorothy's Desire to See the Host

This spouse [of Christ] was so attached to the life-giving odor of the sacrament that from infancy to the end of her life she experienced a great desire to look upon the most holy host. It sometimes happened that she gazed upon the host a hundred times in a single day, and yet she desired to see it even more often. . . . Accompanying this desire to look upon Christ's body was also the desire to receive this body several times a year; from the time she was eleven her ardent wish was to receive it seven times a year but, since she was a child, she was permitted to do so only twice each year. When she grew up, her desire increased and she received Christ's body seven times a year and often a little more frequently after her marriage. Even though the times she received Christ's body during the year increased, yet this intense desire—so fervent, holy, and pious—to receive the longed-for sacrament did not subside or diminish. Rather, it grew to such an extent that she passed nights without sleep. As a result, she arranged her affairs so that she was able to go to church early in the morning where, at the celebration of the morning Mass, she could at least look upon the host her heart so greatly desired. And her hunger for this food was often so strong and so great that, when she was permitted to receive, she liked to snatch with her mouth the host from the priest's hands. More than once it happened that she was so carried away before the elevation that she remained in ecstasy till afterwards. And thus she did not see the host . . .

Jean de Marienwerder, Septillium, St. Dorothy of Danzig d. 1394, III, ch. 2.

78

Popular Devotion and the Liturgy of the Mass

Popular understanding believed that looking at the sacrament brought about the same benefits as communion itself. It was not rare, therefore, for the faithful to leave church immediately after the elevation, which was the source of spiritual grace and even earthly assistance. Some think that the legend of the Holy Grail was a symbolic expression of this belief, in which a person is saved by looking at the sacred vessel. In any case, popular piety sometimes assumed aberrant forms. In some places people thought a Christian's life could be extended in proportion to the time spent looking at the body of Christ. As a result, Christians requested that the length of the elevation be prolonged. As a consequence, the host was often placed in a reliquary in a niche located above the altar throughout the whole Mass. These sentiments and practice contributed to the development of the cult of the blessed sacrament. The eucharistic bread is exposed in a "monstrance, or "ostensorium," throughout the liturgy of the hours, and carried solemnly through the streets in processions that greatly attracted medieval crowds.

Benefits Gained from Looking at the Host

Indeed happy is the person who once each day can look upon the body of God. For this brings about so much good that, as St. Augustine teaches, on the day you behold you will certainly obtain the following benefits: food and drink according to your needs, and no one will quarrel with you as to these; God will pardon you useless oaths and words; you will not have to fear sudden death on this day. I promise you that on this day you will not loose your sight, and each step that you take for this purpose will be counted as useful when you have need of this.

John Myre, Instructions for parish priests
(14th century)

The multiplication of private Masses favored these developments. Outside the space reserved for pontifical, chapter, or conventual celebrations, a space often surrounded with dark walls, the gothic edifices contained a large nave surrounded by a multitude of chapels, each having an altar set back against the wall. In these alcoves Masses were "read" or "said" by priests, whose main job throughout most of the morning was here. Devout Christians hurried from one altar to another, assisting at as many elevations as possible to obtain graces of all kinds. Further, during

A Theologian Reacts

Christ's body is not received by being seen, but only its sacrament, because sight does not penetrate to the substance of Christ's body, but only to the sacramental species . . . But he who eats, receives not only the sacramental species, but likewise Christ Himself Who is under them. Consequently, no one is forbidden to behold Christ's body, when once he has received Christ's sacrament, namely, Baptism: whereas the non-baptized are not to be allowed even to see this sacrament, as is clear from Dionysius (*Eccl. Hier. vii*). But only those are to be allowed to share in the eating who are united with Christ not merely sacramentally, but likewise really.

St. Thomas, Summa Theologica, part 3, quest. 80, art. 4, response to the 4th objection.

A Protestant Complaint

In various areas of England the rustics in the countryside cry out to the priest: "Higher, Sire John, higher, raise it a little higher."

Displaying of the Popish Mass (Parker Society, III, p. 270)

the fourteenth and fifteenth centuries miracle stories concerning the eucharistic bread brought crowds of pilgrims on the run: hosts that cure, the infant Jesus appearing in the hands of the priest, and other tales were widespread.

Not only the people's understanding of the eucharist but also their knowledge of Jesus was transformed by these new attitudes. No longer was the Mass the prayer of Christ who draws people into his saving death and resurrection for the glory of God the Father. Now Christians were, so to say, face to face with God the Savior; but Jesus' mission as mediator fades from view the more his presence is confined to the static sacred species that can be seen but not touched. In France, the Feast of God is the title given to the solemnity of *Corpus Christi*, instituted by Urban V in 1264, just as one speaks of the "Good God" in regard to the well-known statue of the Savior in the cathedral of Amiens. As the humanity of the Savior receded, the importance accorded to the intercession of Our Lady and the saints grew exponentially as intermediaries between the divinity and believers. The saints filled the gap created when the mediation of the one Son was forgotten. The formula "to Jesus through Mary" is substituted in some cases for the ancient profession of Christian faith: "to the Father through the Son."

Chapels multiplied in the churches, and these chapels were not only for private Masses; each was dedicated to the heavenly patron of the fraternity, guild, or family entrusted with its upkeep, and this patron's image dominated the altar. At the far end of the apse was the altar, now elevated in imitation of the holy of holies in the ancient temple at Jerusalem. The high altar accommodated the tabernacle. Bishops and theologians tried to no avail to restrain excesses and focus the people's attention on the true meaning of the blessed sacrament and veneration of the saints, but the enthusiasm of popular devotion pays no attention.

A further decadence of liturgical spirituality occurred in the fourteenth century. Meditation on Christ's passion was accompanied by excessively realistic representations of Christ Crucified and the "Sorrowful Mother"; such meditation also prompted allegorical commentaries on the ceremonies of the Mass. Episodes of the stations of the cross were discovered, for example, in the Mass. The priest wearing the chasuble was thought to represent Jesus clothed with the garment of derision; crossing from one side of the altar to the other suggests the tribunal of Caiphas at the praetorium of Pilate; the washing of hands recalls the Roman procurator's action the night Jesus died. In fact, the very meaning of the sacrament was threatened; the Mass was approached as a type of mime or sacred drama. Stage pieces, or "mysteries," and living tableaux were developed as

An Allegorical Commentary by the Future Pope Innocent III

The Eucharistic Prayer

The sacred words must not be profaned. If everyone knows these words because all have heard them, then these words can be repeated in public and in profane places. This is why the church has decreed that the priest is to say this prayer secretly, a prayer having the appearance of a mystery. It is said that some shepherds, at a time before this custom was established, repeated these words in the fields and thus were struck down by God.

In the Mysteries we make memory of the passion, namely, of what occurred during the week before the Passover, from the tenth day of the first lunar month when Jesus entered Jerusalem, till the seventeenth day when he was raised from the dead. This is why most sacramentaries contain a picture of Christ's image between the preface and the canon; we are not merely to understand the text but also to contemplate the image which inspires the memory of the Lord's passion. Perhaps it is the result more of Providence than of human art that the Canon begins with the letter T, a letter whose form is that of a cross and which symbolizes a cross. In fact, the T recalls the mystery of the cross since God says through the prophet: "Mark with a tau the foreheads of those who lament and cry" (Ez 9:4).

Te igitur clementissime Pater. The true Lamb entered Jerusalem on the very day when the crowds acclaimed Christ. This was the tenth day of the first lunar month, the day when the Law called for the Hebrews to take into their homes the symbolic lamb. Spied upon by those men, full of hate, men who stirred up the people, he was threatened by the snares intended to cause his death. There were three who handed Christ over: God, Judas, and the Jew . . . To express this the priest makes three crosses over the gifts as he says: *Haec dona, haec munera, haec sacrificia illibata.* He was handed over by God like a gift, by Judas on behalf of those who were present, by the Jew as a sacrifice without stain. It was unto "death, death on a cross" (Phil 2:8) that he was handed over by each of the three . . .

Lotario Conti (pope in 1198),
De sacro altaris mysterio, liber III, 1-3

82

accompaniments to preaching. Such religious theater assumed even greater prominence in the first half of the fifteenth century.

Missals at the End of the Middle Ages

Various expansive actions and postures well-suited to express the dramatic nature of the liturgy were added to the private prayers of the priest and his ministers. In addition, though the whole Latin (western) world followed essentially the same liturgy, yet in the thirteenth century each diocese established its own customs and had its own diocesan missal. The mendicant orders likewise adopted a common practice within each particular order. Then as the members of these orders wend their way throughout Christendom, they continue to offer the Mass according to the practice of their order, thus creating at least a semblance of unity: the Dominicans spread the main elements of Parisian usage; the Carmelites, the rite that had been established in the patriarchate of Jerusalem; and the Franciscans, in turn, propagate the customs of the Roman Curia. The missal used by the friars, in fact, very probably derived from a pontifical ordinary dating from the first half of the thirteenth century.

We should mention, however, that a commentary on the Mass written in Rome at the end of the twelfth century belies these developments: it distinguished the ceremonies proper to a bishop from those proper to priests, provided for communion to be distributed under both forms, and included only two private prayers: the psalm *Iudica me* and the "I confess" at the beginning of the celebration.

The first printed Roman Missal, published in 1474, propagated the usages received from the Franciscans. Numerous editions of this missal will appear in the years to follow. In this way it prepares for the unification of the liturgy in the West, a unification that only occurs after the Council of Trent.

Questions Regarding the Consecration

The elevation of the host focused attention on the institution narrative and even—as we have shown—isolated this narrative from the rest of the eucharistic prayer. Medieval theology, furthermore, seemed to sanction this state of affairs, and the Reformers, meaning no doubt to restore the traditional integrity of the Mass, omitted saying these words over the bread and the wine. The churches of the East, for their part, considered the epiclesis as the essential element of the consecration. This engendered a lively controversy, though not during the ninth to eleventh centuries, a time when controversy existed between Rome and Constantinople.

In the fourteenth century the noted liturgist Nicholas Cabasilas, realizing the opposition between Rome and his own church, undertook to justify it. In 1439 the question is debated at the Council of Florence, and the Byzantines are requested for an official oral declaration on the matter. The council's initial decree specified that it is only through the words of Christ that the consecration takes place. But Pope Eugene IV removed this phrase from the text that was to be signed so as not to insult the eastern Christians by having them believe that they had been holding a contrary opinion till now. His action affirmed the doctrine and yet recognized that the liturgical usages of the two churches (the Greeks also depend on liturgical practice to defend their position) cannot resolve a question that was not posed in these terms when the prayers were composed.

Further Reading

Robert Cabié, *The Mass* 136-148.

Joseph Jungmann, *The Mass of the Roman Rite* (1 volume edition) 77-96.

Nathan Mitchell, *Cult and Controversy: The Worship of the Eucharist outside Mass* (New York: Pueblo Publishing Company, 1982) 44-128.

Herman Wegman, *Christian Worship in East and West* 204-238.

Chapter VII

The Missal of Saint Pius V
XVI century

The Council of Trent and the Reform of the Mass

At the beginning of the sixteenth century many pastors felt that a reform was needed. The task was urgent to counteract popular customs that were often attached to superstition and to give some order to the multitude of secondary formulas and gestures that impeded the faithful's grasp of the essential mystery of the eucharist.

In this mind a number of bishops attended the council convoked at Trent by Paul III in 1545. Without question such a reformist tendency character-ized their debates in the sessions that continued till 1563. But the context of this assembly, the Reformation, forced them to do battle on two fronts simultaneously. The bishops certainly had to oppose the abuses that Luther and his disciples were, obligingly enough, denouncing; and yet, the excesses of those who rejected Catholic doctrine suggested to the bishops that doctrinal clarity and caution were more pressing needs.

For this reason, the bishops put aside the use of the vernacular lest they give credence to the Protestants' arguments in favor of using the language of the people. The disadvantages of using Latin could be remedied, the bishops said, by interventions during the celebration. The same concern for prudence and pastoral care marked their directions in regard to reserving the eucharist, communion to the sick, communion of children, and the giving of the chalice to the laity. The council's doctrinal decisions on the Mass coincided with reform decrees so that "the spirit of the faithful [may] be stimulated through visible signs full of religion and piety, for the

"The sheep of Christ are not to go unfed"

Although the Mass contains much instruction for the faithful, the Fathers did not think it should be celebrated in the vernacular indiscriminately. Therefore, the ancient rite of each Church, approved by the holy Roman Church, the mother and teacher of all the Churches, being everywhere maintained, the holy Council, in order that the sheep of Christ may not go unfed, lest "the children beg for food but no one gives it to them" (Lam 4:4), orders that pastors and all who have the care of souls must frequently, either by themselves or through others, explain during the celebration of Masses some of the readings of the Mass and among other things give some instruction about the mystery of the most holy sacrifice, especially on Sundays and feastdays.

Council of Trent, Session 22, ch. 8 (September 1562)

Martin Luther on the Words of the Mass

The whole power of the mass consists in the words of Christ, in which he testifies that forgiveness of sins is bestowed on all those who believe that his body is given and his blood poured out for them. This is why nothing is more important for those who go to hear mass than to ponder these words diligently and in full faith. Unless they do this, all else that they do is in vain. This is surely true, that to every promise of his, God usually adds some sign as a memorial or remembrance of the promise, so that thereby we may serve him more diligently and he may admonish us more effectually . . . in every promise of God two things are presented to us, the words and the sign, so that we are to understand the word to be the testament, but the sign to be the sacrament. Thus, in the mass, the word of Christ is the testament, and the bread and wine are the sacrament. And as there is greater power in the word than in the sign, so there is greater power in the testament than in the sacrament; for a man can have and use the word or testament apart from the sign or sacrament . . . .

Martin Luther, The Babylonian Captivity of the Church

86

Pope Pius V Promulgates the Tridentine Missal

. . . the Council of Trent reserved to us the publication and correction of the holy books, of the catechism, the missal, and the breviary; once, thanks to God, the catechism for the formation of the people, and the corrected breviary for the celebration of the praise due to God were published, it appeared necessary for us to consider immediately what remained to be done in this area, namely, the publication of the missal so that it correspond to the breviary, as is right and fitting, just as it is desirable that in the church of God there be one manner of saying the office and one single rite for celebrating Mass. This is why we entrusted this work to men chosen for their learning. They closely compared everything with the ancient manuscripts found in the Vatican Library and with other manuscripts, corrected and incorrupt, collected from all over; they consulted the writings of those ancient and trustworthy authors who have left us information concerning the holy arrangement of these rites, and they restored the rites of the Mass to the form received from the holy Fathers. Having examined and checked this, and after full consideration, we have ordered that the Missal be published at Rome as soon as possible . . . so that the usages of the holy Roman Church, mother and teacher of all other churches, be adopted and observed by all . . . We prescribe and order by this declaration, whose force is perpetual, that all the churches relinquish the use of their proper missals . . .; exceptions are made for a rite approved at its origin by the Apostolic See or for a custom faithfully observed by these churches for at least two hundred years for the celebration of Mass; it is not our intention to suppress in any way such a rite or custom.

Bull, Quo primum tempore (19 July 1570)

contemplation of the invisible realities hidden in this sacrifice" (22nd session [1562] ch. 5). Meanwhile, the council entrusted the task of publishing the new missal to the pope.

Pius IV began the reform project by establishing a commission; unfortunately its working notes are no longer available, and in 1565 Pius IV died. Five years later, his successor, Pius V, published the *Roman Missal Restored by the Decree of the Council of Trent*, together with its *General Rubrics* and the *Rite to be Observed in the Celebration of Mass*.

The Spirit of the New Missal

Pius V best expressed the spirit of the reform. It was to be a return to the sources, a return beyond medieval liturgical innovations to discover the tradition of the early church. Pius V was, in fact, a courageous innovator, and the remarkable paradox is that his name is invoked by those who oppose the similar reform initiated by Vatican II. The pope removed a large number of feastdays from the calendar that had become so overloaded that the celebration of Sunday was obscured. He suppressed most of the sequences, organized the prayers that are always said silently, and simplified the priest's gestures by excluding accretions that stemmed from excessive devotion. He removed from the musical repertoire all compositions extraneous to the liturgy, some of which even encroached on the Canon. And above all, Pius V discouraged any attempt at superstition on the part of the people.

Nevertheless, the Missal of 1570 did not fulfill expectations. The commission entrusted with the project had to work very quickly, and had no access to the kind of scientific work that appeared the following century. As a result, the Missal of Pius V is merely a new tributary of the 1474 Missal of the Curia. The rites could have undergone greater simplification, and one can imagine the result, if, for example, in place of the Franciscan model, the missal of the Carthusians had been followed, which by the way survived after 1570 with the liturgical usages of the Dominicans, the Carmelites, and several local churches.

The unification of the liturgy, promoted by the invention of printing, was surely what the pope had in mind when he stated that nothing was ever to be changed in this missal which he was imposing on the whole West; he wanted, above all, to avoid any return to the constant alterations that had taken place in the medieval period, and to ensure a certain degree of stability. The text was never intended to forbid any future changes made by the same authority. The two later editions of the Tridentine book, the one appearing in 1604 under Clement VIII; the other, in 1634 under Urban VIII, had no scruples in incorporating modifications, not to mention the edition of Pius X, who in 1914 approved even more important changes.

The Mass: Sung and Read

The "conventual" Mass, celebrated with all the regular clergy or religious present, is the Tridentine norm and model for parishes where, at least on Sunday, enough ministers can be found among the laity to ensure a certain degree of solemnity. By contrast, there is also the "read" or "low" Mass, namely, the Mass without singing. We must grasp this distinction if we are to understand the structure of the Mass in the Tridentine Missal. In both cases the priest follows the same rubrics and says the same words. But when the Mass is sung, its sung parts give the liturgical action a relief that clearly distinguishes the secondary nature of the private prayers.

The Entrance Rites

In the Missal of Pius V, the Mass, when sung, begins with the psalm known as the *Introit*. This psalm has been reduced to a single verse followed by a doxology; an antiphon with a florid melody is sung before and after the verse. This music is meager but adequate for the procession of the ministers. When they arrive at the foot of the altar they quietly say Psalm 43 as they respond to one another: "I will go unto the altar of God, to God who gives joy to my youth"; the "I confess" and several shorter prayers follow. These prayers were originally said while the ministers walked from the sacristy to the sanctuary, but the distance to the sanctuary is now very short. At low Masses everything begins with the recitation of these prayers. The priest then goes up to the altar and says the prayer *Aufer a nobis*. Although this text appears in old Roman sources, it was not used for this purpose until the eleventh century. Then the priest kisses the altar; as he does so, he says a prayer alluding to the relics of the saints contained therein. If it is a solemn Mass, the first incensation now takes place, with a formula accompanying the blessing of the incense.

The schola sings the *Kyrie eleison* and then, if it occurs, the *Gloria in excelsis*. The missal is placed on the south side of the altar in churches that face the east. After greeting the assembly, the priest sings the *Collects*; frequently there are many, since prayers from another office (Lauds or Vespers, or others) or recommending a particular intention may be added to the prayer of the day.

The Liturgy of the Word

The first reading is called the *epistle* although it is not always taken from the letters of the apostles. It is read by the priest on the same side while it is chanted by the subdeacon or a reader. Standing at the north side of the altar, the priest sings the *gospel* or reads it at the same time the deacon is singing it: it is set off by two formulas: "Purify my heart and my lips . . ." and "May the words of the gospel take away our sins." Each reading is followed by a response given quietly by a cleric: *Deo gratias, Laus tibi, Christe.* The people, not knowing Latin, are less responsive to the word of God than they are to the words and gestures surrounding it, especially those occurring before the gospel. These embellishments consist of the initial acclamation, coming from the Gallican liturgy ("Glory to you, O Lord"); the signs of the cross traced on the book and on oneself; and the incensation of the book.

The *Gradual*, occurring between the two readings, has here lost its responsorial form. The *Alleluia* verse is accompanied by a text that is not always taken from the psalms or even from the Bible; during Lent the Alleluia is replaced by the *Tract*, a section of a psalm without a refrain.

The Missal of Pius V suppresses almost all the sequences, except the *Victimae paschali* at Easter, the *Veni sancte Spiritus* at Pentecost, the *Lauda Sion* at Corpus Christi, and the *Dies irae* at Masses for the dead. The *Stabat Mater* is not part of the Roman liturgy until the eighteenth century when a local feast in honor of Our Lady of Sorrows was extended to the whole church.

The missal of 1570 does not mention the homily, but if the priest is to preach, he removes his chasuble and descends into the nave where the pulpit is located; preaching easily assumes a life of its own, a life independent of the celebration.

On Sundays and feasts the creed is sung. The *oremus*, or "let us pray," that follows is a vestige of the general prayer; the prayer itself having disappeared long ago.

The Offertory

At the offertory numerous private prayers accompany the actions of the minister, in anticipation of the Canon. Although only bread and wine are on the altar, the priest speaks of the "spotless victim," the "cup of salvation," and about the offering of sacrifice. Elements of the anamnesis, the beginnings of an epiclesis, and even intercessions for the living and the dead are included in these prayers. As water is poured into the chalice, the priest says a formula inspired by an ancient Christmas collect. An old

Private Prayers during the Offertory

The priest takes the paten with the host and offers it while saying:

Receive, Holy Father, God almighty and everlasting, this unblemished host which I, your unworthy servant, offer to you, my living and true God, for my own countless sins, offenses, and failings; for all here present and for all faithful Christians, living and dead, that it may help both me and them unto salvation in life eternal. Amen.

The priest mixes water with the wine and blesses it while saying:

O God, in a wonderful way you created and ennobled human nature, and still more wonderfully renewed it. Grant us that by the mystery of this water and wine we may share in the Godhead of him who chose to share in our manhood: Jesus Christ your Son, our Lord, who lives and . . .

The priest and the deacon take the chalice and offer it while saying:

We offer you the cup of salvation, Lord, asking your mercy that it may ascend as a sweet fragrance in the presence of your divine majesty: for our salvation and that of the whole world. Amen.

He makes a sign of the cross with the chalice, places it on the altar, and says while bowing:

Humble in spirit and repentant in heart, may we be accepted by you, O Lord, and may our sacrifice be so offered in your sight this day that it may be pleasing to you, Lord, God.

He stands erect and says:

Come, you who make holy, God everlasting and almighty, and bless this sacrifice made ready for your holy name.

>>>>>

He washes his hands as he says:
I will wash my hands among the innocent, and will go round your altar, O Lord. That I may hear the sound of your praise, and tell of all your wondrous deeds. Lord, I have loved the beauty of your house, and the place where your glory dwells. O God, do not destroy my soul with the wicked, nor my life with men of blood. Their hands are stained with crimes, and their right hand is filled with gifts. But as for me, I have walked in innocence; redeem me and have mercy on me. My foot has stood in the right path; I will praise you, O Lord, in the assemblies.

He bows and says:
Receive, O Holy Trinity, this offering which we make to you in remembrance of the passion, resurrrection and ascension of our Lord Jesus Christ, and in honor of blessed Mary, ever Virgin, of blessed John the Baptist, the holy apostles Peter and Paul, of these and of all the saints; that it may avail to their honor and our salvation. May they be pleased to pray for us in heaven, whose memory we now keep on earth: through the same Christ our Lord. Amen.

He stands upright and says:
Brethren, pray that my sacrifice and yours may become acceptable to God the Father almighty.

The response:
May the Lord accept the sacrifice from your hands, unto the praise and glory of his name, for our advantage and that of all his holy Church.

rubric is misinterpreted that turns this formula into a blessing. On the other hand, protestations of humility and repentance are not absent, for example, Psalm 26 is said while the celebrant washes his hands. The *Orate fratres* belongs to the same *genre*: the priest recommends himself to the prayer of the other ministers; their response repeats the same theme.

These texts had already appeared, with variations and in different sequences, in numerous diocesan missals of the Middle Ages.

The incensation of the gifts, the altar, and the priest, which is the oldest and most important incensation in the Roman Mass did not originate in Rome, where it was customary simply to carry burning incense in a pan. Incensing the altar and the priest was a sign of honor of Carolingian origin that had become quite widespread by the eleventh century. Soon it was accompanied by words said by the minister and extended to all the clergy who were present.

While all of this is taking place, the schola sings the Offertory, which has been reduced to a single verse. The prayer over the gifts, having become a silent prayer, the *Secret*, is itself said quietly till its conclusion: *Per omnia saecula saeculorum.*

The Canon

After the singing of the preface, the *Sanctus* often overlaps the eucharistic prayer. At times it is even resumed after the elevation which is highlighted by the ringing of bells. Solemn Masses included a procession of clerics carrying candles and the swinging of censers. The priest's silent prayer is encumbered with numerous signs of the cross made over the gifts or on himself, with inclinations and genuflections. The conclusion of the final doxology is always given in a loud voice so that the *Amen* might resound, but this acclamation is no longer made by everyone, as was true in ancient times.

The Our Father, the Peace, and the Fraction

After the Canon, various elements infringe one on the other: the bread is broken before the end of the prayer that follows the Our Father, and the *Agnus Dei*, which originally accompanied the fraction, now separates the kiss of peace from the presider's wish that "the peace of the Lord be with you always." Various postures and actions added during the medieval period characterize these rites.

Since the eleventh century the *Libera*, the embolism, or embellishment, after the Our Father, has been said silently, though it was chanted at Milan and Lyons and at Mass on Holy Saturday.

From the "Our Father" to the Communion

* = said aloud

The priest alone. * Let us pray: Taught by our Savior's command and informed by the word of God we make bold to say: Our Father . . . and lead us not into temptation.
BUT DELIVER US FROM EVIL.

He breaks the bread over the chalice and detaches a particle. We ask you, O Lord, to free us from all evils, past, present and to come. By the prayers of the blessed and glorious Mary, ever Virgin, Mother of God, and of your blessed apostles Peter and Paul, and Andrew, and of all the saints, mercifully grant peace in our days. Through your mercy's help may we always be free from sin and safe from all distress through . . .
* for ever and ever.
AMEN.

He places the particle in the chalice. * May the peace of the Lord be always with you.
AND WITH YOU ALSO.
LAMB OF GOD, YOU WHO TAKE AWAY THE SINS OF THE WORLD, HAVE MERCY ON US. (twice) LAMB OF GOD . . . GRANT US PEACE.
Lord Jesus Christ who said to your apostles: "Peace I leave with you, my peace I give to you," do not look upon my sins, but upon the faith of your Church. Please grant her peace and unity according to your will: you who are God living and reigning . . .
At solemn Masses the clergy exchange the peace.

Then the priest says: Lord Jesus Christ, Son of the living God, according to the will of the Father and through the help

>>>>>

94

of the Holy Spirit you gave life to the world by your death. By this your most holy Body and Blood deliver me from all my sins and from all evils. Make me always cling to your commandments and never let me be separated from you who with the same God . . .

Let not the sharing of your Body, O Lord Jesus Christ, which I unworthy make bold to receive, become my judgment and condemnation. But through your goodness may it be my safeguard and a healing remedy . . .

I will take the bread of heaven and call upon the name of the Lord. Lord, I am not worthy that you should come under my roof; say but the word and my soul shall be healed (three times).

The priest receives the consecrated bread. May the Body of our Lord Jesus Christ keep my spirit unto life everlasting.

What shall I return to the Lord for all that he has given to me? I will take the cup of salvation. I will call on the name of the Lord, singing his praise. "I will call upon the Lord and I shall be saved from my enemies."

The priest receives from the chalice. May the Body of our Lord Jesus Christ keep my spirit unto life everlasting. Amen.

After the "Confiteor," "Misereatur," and "Indulgentiam," the priest shows the body of Christ. Behold the Lamb of God, behold him who takes away the sins of the world.

LORD, I AM NOT WORTHY . . . (three times).

The priest distributes communion. May the Body of our Lord Jesus Christ keep your spirit unto life everlasting. Amen.

No longer does the kiss of peace have its original form as a mutual greeting, among all the participants. At first it was restricted to those who would receive the eucharist; but now it concerns only the clergy: the deacon receives it from the priest who has kissed the altar; and then the deacon "carries" it to the rows of clerics who pass it along to one another. In some cases a "pax board" was used, namely, an ornamental plaque that each person kissed in turn.

The fraction has lost its essential meaning since the priest himself consumes the two portions of the bread he has broken. The use of very small hosts, cut out beforehand for the communion of the faithful, is partially the cause for this anomaly.

The Communion

The celebrant prepares himself for communion by saying three prayers written in the first person singular. The first, "Lord Jesus Christ, you said to your apostles . . .," precedes the kiss of peace; it first appeared in Germany at the beginning of the eleventh century. The second was more widespread in the Middle Ages, it is found in the ninth-century Sacramentary of Amiens: "Lord Jesus Christ, Son of the living God . . ." The third prayer originated in the tenth century: "May this communion in your body and blood . . ." These prayers first appeared in collections used by the laity. As the celebrant receives the consecrated bread and wine, he says other prayers taken from the psalms or the Gospel.

For the communion of the faithful, the Missal of Pius V retains the ritual borrowed from the rite of the sick. The missal presumes that the hosts received by those who approach the holy table were consecrated at the same Mass, but this prescription was rarely observed. The sacrament was reserved from previous Masses. The connection between the eucharistic action and the bread was no longer visible in the symbol. The ancient communion psalm was also reduced to a single verse with an ornate melody. However brief, it sufficed to fill up the time during which only a small number of people received communion.

The formulas *Quod ore sumpsimus* and *Corpus tuum quod sumpsi* accompany the purification of the chalice. The former comes from old Roman books; the latter from the Gallican tradition: both were for the private devotion of the faithful before being appropriated for use within the liturgy of the Mass.

The *Postcommunion*, like the collect and secret, could be followed by a series of orations. Then the assembly is dismissed by the deacon, if one is present, who uses the *Ite missa est*. But competing with this formula is another text that seems to have come from ancient Gallican usage and which was used, according to the rubrics of the eleventh century, each time the celebration did not include the *Gloria in excelsis*; at Masses for the dead the invitation to depart is replaced by a banal *Requiescant in pace*. The blessing bestowed by the priest is a late element; from the thirteenth century onward its wording varies; and we cannot tell whether it was originally intended to be an act of devotion, after everything else was completed, or whether it was to be considered an integral part of the Mass, as we find in the Missal of Pius V.

The beginning of John's Gospel was originally the celebrant's private meditation after Mass, but the custom arose whereby he recited it while leaving the sanctuary (as the bishop did after the pontifical Mass till recent reforms). Therefore, in the thirteenth century, the text came to be said at the altar except at the bishop's Mass. This practice was retained by the Tridentine Missal.

Concelebration

In the west bishops and priests concelebrated only at the Mass of their ordination. The church at Lyons, however, retained a custom that seems to have been widespread in the Middle Ages: it occurs on Holy Thursday, when all the priests participate in and receive from the bishop the consecrated oils. The collegial character of the blessing of oil brings about a collegiality in praying the Canon, within which the blessing is inserted. The rubrics call for each concelebrant to say all the prayers of the Mass. The ceremonial has undergone all kinds of modifications; the priests, for example, kneel and receive the eucharist only under the form of bread.

The notion of concelebration was much more widespread in the East; but starting with the seventeenth century, the Russians at least were influenced by the Latin theology that required the common recitation of the principal parts of the anaphora.

* * * *

Pius V allowed a time interval, different according to the distance of individual churches from Rome, before his decisions had to be enacted. Though it took more time than anticipated, his Missal rather quickly succeeded in giving the rites of the Mass a renewed form which, throughout several centuries, will characterize the style of the Roman liturgy and spread to all continents. Renewal, however, is a relative term. The contributions of the Middle Ages, as we have seen, enriched various parts of the celebration; the reform sufficed merely to gather these together, once

Thoughts on the Tridentine Reform

Does not the church do the same things everywhere? What is done in Rome, is this not what is done in France, in Germany, in Poland, in the Indies, and elsewhere? Do we not find the same sacrifice, the same sacraments, the same ceremonies, and even the same language all over? Although from the beginning criticism was raised in regard to celebrating in an language no one understood, the church—having given consideration to all things and having compared this difficulty with the problems that would arise if each country celebrated Mass in its own language—desires that there be unanimity and uniformity in all things so as to maintain one spirit. In spite of the complaints put forth, the church desires that each country accomodate itself to the customs established by the church. What is the reason for this? God is honored when everyone does things the same way. Furthermore, conformity helps avoid great abuses. If only you could have seen the diversity—I do not wish to speak of the ugliness—in the Mass as celebrated some forty years ago. It would have made you feel ashamed. It seems to me that there was nothing more unbecoming in the world than the various ways in which the Mass was celebrated. Some began the Mass with the *Pater noster*; others held the chasuble while saying the *Introibo* and then putting on the vestment. Once I was at Saint-Germain-en-Laye where I saw seven or eight priests all saying Mass differently: one doing it one way, another doing it another way: it was a variety worthy of tears. But take heart. We should praise God that in his divine goodness he was pleased to remedy, little by little, this great disorder. Unfortunately, this disorder has not completely disappeared. Numerous differences in the celebration of the holy mysteries still exist. There are still many ill-formed priests who have not instructed themselves or who do not wish to observe that uniformity brought about by following the rubrics.

Vincent de Paul, Conference of May 23 1659; ed. P. Coste, vol. 12 (Paris: Gabalda, 1924) 258-259.

they were purified of their more debatable features. Because of circumstances the reform could not respond fully to the intentions of those who initiated it; in the centuries that followed many clamored for a bolder revision. It is, moreover, interesting to wonder just how the Christian people really experienced the eucharist during the 400-year period in which the priests were using the book Pius V revised for the Council of Trent.

Further Reading

Robert Cabié, *The Eucharist* 149-171.
Joseph Jungmann, *The Mass of the Roman Rite* (1 volume edition) 96-105.
Cheslyn Jones and others, eds., *The Study of Liturgy* 241-244.
Theodor Klauser, *A Short History of the Western Liturgy* 124-129.
R. Theisen, "The Reform of the Mass Liturgy and the Council of Trent," *Worship* 40 (November 1966) 565-583.

Chapter VIII

Popular Devotion to the Holy Sacrifice of the Mass
XVI-XX century

If the Council of Trent's work on the Mass was to be both pastoral and unifying, its official implementation in Christian worship seems to have been more honored in the second than in the first of these two aspects. The liturgy, with its suspect features now removed, is carefully regulated by a body of rubrics whose precise details are increasingly governed by the Congregation of Rites, a papal department that Sixtus V established in 1588. The liturgy became the concern of specialists only. To avoid every danger of superstition the celebration of Mass had to be entirely separate from the excesses of popular religion that were so characteristic of the Middle Ages and that appeared again under new forms during the Romantic period.

These concerns notwithstanding, the prayer of the church cannot be understood on the basis of its books. The vitality of ritual prescriptions and codification depends on the ritual's incorporation into the life and concrete experience of communities who integrate the prescriptions and established customs.

On the other hand, the reform movement undertaken at the end of the sixteenth century and at the beginning of the seventeenth century— Charles Borromeo, the archbishop of Milan is an outstanding figure in this era—was sensitive to the unbelief among the masses, which it attributed not to their will but to their ignorance of religion. And, with remarkable pastoral care, these reformers initiate a program of instruction. Parish missions, educational institutions for the young, and seminaries for the formation of the clergy multiply. Liturgical life, in spite of difficulties, is part of this effort: bishops and priests use every means to understand and guide the yearnings of popular piety.

The parish Sunday Mass is an important moment of a Christian's life. In the seventeenth century there is still only one Mass in each church, at least in towns and villages. The hour for this celebration is determined by diocesan or synod statutes, and the celebration can be quite lengthy. Rites found in the ceremonials published by the authority of the bishop are added to those prescribed by the missal.

> ### Jean de la Fontaine at a Parish Mass
>
> On Sunday we set out early in the morning. Madame C. and our aunt accompanied us as far as Bourg-la-Reine. We waited there for almost three hours; and, to occupy ourselves, or to bore ourselves less (I really don't know which I should say), we heard the parish Mass. The procession, the blessed water, the prone, nothing was lacking. We were fortunate in that the curate was ignorant and did not preach.
>
> *Letter to his wife, August 30, 1663*

First, a blessing of water is added. According to the Roman rubrics, this blessing takes place in the sacristy, but in France the water is blessed in the choir or nave, and, as Pierre LeBrun remarks in the eighteenth century, "this custom seems to give pleasure to the people." Then came the sprinkling, which was often prolonged by a procession of the ministers throughout the church. These ritual customs are a transposition of ancient monastic practice: at dawn on Sunday, the hour at which the holy women had found the tomb empty, religious monks and nuns performed a lustration, a cleansing, of the cloister and of all places within the monastery. Joining these practices to the parish Mass emphasizes the dominical character of the day.

The prescriptions of the Tridentine Missal are modified in the celebration that follows: laity can take the place of clerics when the latter are absent; appointed singers, often garbed in cassock and surplice, sing Gregorian melodies that have been revised and corrected according to the taste of the times; they sometimes also proclaim the epistle; others — very often young boys — serve at the altar.

The prone is inserted after the gospel. In time this element will often be confused with the sermon, but in fact the prone contains a series of

102

An Example of Prayers of the Prone

Knowing that God is pleased with prayer that comes from a contrite and humble heart, we offer to him our very humble prayers, that he may teach us to do his holy will. Not only today & during the present week but also throughout our whole lives may we be enabled to give him pleasing service, & standing firm on the foundation of a true faith, may we be able to have a holy hope of our salvation by keeping his commandments with the help of his grace.

We also pray for the peace and unity of the church, for the growth of the Catholic, apostolic & Roman faith, for the eradication of heresies, for the conversion of the infidels, of heretics, of schismatics, & of all those who are separated from this faith, that God be recognized, served, & adored everywhere.

We pray for all prelates & pastors of the church, & in particular for our Holy Father the Pope and for the Most Reverend Father in God Bishop N., our own prelate, and for all pastors in charge of souls, that God give them the grace to fulfill their ministry as to lead themselves and the people entrusted to them in the way of salvation so that they attain eternal life.

We also pray for the peace & tranquility of this kingdom, for the unity of Christian princes & in particular for our most Christian king & and for the whole royal family, for all magistrates and officials who govern us under him & especially for the Lord (or the Lady) of this place, that by their authority, their advice, and their good example, they lead us to the exact observance of the commandments of God and of the church & keep us in good peace.

We pray for all the benefactors of this church, in particular for those who today offer the blessed bread, for those who make the offerings & for those who have given of their goods to adorn and maintain this church, that God, by his goodness & kindness consent to reward them in this world & in the next,

>>>>>

We pray for all women who are widows, for orphans, & for all who are sick in any way, for captives and the afflicted, that God might console them & deliver them from their afflictions or give them patience in their sufferings.

We pray for pregnant women, that God sustain them & enable them to bring their fruit to the holy font of baptism.

We pray for all who are in the state of grace, that God keep them there, & for those who are in mortal sin, that, having been enlightened and converted by his grace, they recognize their sins & undertake true penitence.

We also pray for all our parents and for all our friends who are absent & who are travelling; may God keep them from every kind of danger & return them to their homes in joy and health.

We also pray for all who belong to this diocese & in particular for those who belong to this parish, that God join them in mutual accord so that they might support one another in love.

Finally, we pray for good weather, that God give us suitable weather for the health of our bodies & and for the conservation of the fruits of the earth, so that when these fruits have been harvested in due season, we might use them for his honor & to aid the poor in their necessities.

For all these intentions & in general for all the intentions the church is accustomed to pray for, we join our wishes & say the following prayers (Ps. 122, verses and three orations).

Since Holy Scripture witnesses & since the church has always believed that it is a holy and salutary thought to pray for the faithful departed, we again offer solemn prayers for them . . . (Ps. 129, verses and two orations, then the Our Father, the Hail Mary, the Creed, and the commandments of God and of the church).

Ritual for the use of the diocese of Alet, 1667

announcements concerning the community, feasts to be celebrated, fasts to be observed, and upcoming social events. The prone is how people learn of royal births, the victories and defeats of armies, and the important decisions of political authorities. The prone also includes a lengthy intercession mentioning diverse intentions; in a way it substitutes for the absent general prayer. Similar compositions are known throughout the Middle Ages, some of them even going back as far as the tenth century. But the Tridentine renewal greatly extends their use, perhaps under the influence of St. Peter Canisius, who in the middle of the sixteenth century composed such a formula. Also included in the prone are the great truths of the faith, under the form of catechetical instruction.

In some places it is customary for the faithful, at the offertory, to process to the entrance of the sanctuary where they venerate the paten with a kiss while placing their offerings on a plate. Even more popular is the rite of the blessed bread, generally offered by members of the assembly and distributed at the end of the celebration. The more Christians are attached to this practice, the less frequently they receive the body of the Lord.

Failure to take communion has become so commonplace that those who wish to receive the eucharist prefer to do so after everyone has left lest they appear pretentious. Much later it will become customary to celebrate a morning "Mass of communion" for these people, and yet this does not usually exempt them from returning for the "High Mass."

Catechesis on the Mass
and the Participation of the Faithful

For many Christians, assisting at Sunday Mass is a custom deeply ingrained among the obligations of social life. Their intentions are pure, but they have few means of entering into the mystery. Often enough what they consider to be the essential aspect of this mystery is an exclusive focus on Christ's presence on the altar.

Meanwhile an extensive pastoral effort is underway to instruct the most fervent of the faithful so that they may truly understand the meaning of the eucharist. Thus Francis de Sales in 1610 invited Philothea to "offer [the Mass] with the priest and the rest of the people. In 1685 F. de Harlay, archbishop of Rouen, writes to the people of his diocese: "Every action of the church is common to the priest and to those assisting; you sacrifice with the priest; and the sacrifice is for you as it is for him." We could quote any number of similar expressions, for example, this one found in a catechism of Montpellier published in 1702: "The Mass is the sacrifice of the people as much as it is the sacrifice of the priest."

How to Hear Mass with Devotion

To hear Mass in a proper manner, either actually or mentally:

1. From the beginning until the priest goes up to the altar, make your preparation with him. This consists in placing yourself in the presence of God, acknowledging your unworthiness, and begging pardon for your sins.

2. From the time he goes up to the altar until the Gospel, consider the birth and life of our Lord in this world, by a simple and general consideration.

3. From the Gospel until after the *Credo*, consider the preaching of our Savior and protest that you resolve to live and die in the faith and obedience of His holy word and in the communion of the holy Catholic Church.

4. From the *Credo* to the *Pater Noster* apply your heart to the mysteries of the Passion and death of our Redeemer. They are essentially represented in this Holy Sacrifice, and with the priest and the rest of the people, you must offer them to God the Father for His honor and for your own salvation.

5. From the *Pater Noster* to the Communion, strive to excite a thousand desires in your heart, ardently wishing to be united forever to our Savior by an everlasting love.

6. From the Communion to the end, return thanks to Jesus Christ for His incarnation, life, Passion, and death; and also for the love He testifies to us in this Holy Sacrifice. Implore him to be forever merciful to you, to your parents, to your friends, and to the whole Church. Humbling yourself with your whole heart, receive devoutly the benediction which our Lord gives you through the ministry of His officer.

Should you prefer to meditate during Mass on the mystery you proposed for your consideration on that day, it is not necessary that you should change your thoughts to make all these particular acts. At the beginning, direct your intention to adore and offer up this Holy Sacrifice by the exercise of your meditations and prayer. In all meditations the aforesaid acts may be found either expressly or tacitly and equivalently.

Francis de Sales, Introduction to the Devout Life

But the conclusion that can be drawn here is that those "assisting" are to pray privately, taking their inspiration from the eucharist itself. No question arises concerning their active participation in the liturgy, as we understand this concept today. Some priests, especially in Jansenist circles, recite the Canon aloud or have the people respond to certain prayers, but such practices are sporadic and are generally reproved by the bishops.

Many French translations of the prayers of the Mass were published between 1597 and 1660, the year when the Assembly of the Clergy condemned the translation of Joseph Voisin. The following year this condemnation is repeated by Alexander VII, who threatened to excommunicate whoever made efforts to have the faithful understand the texts of the Mass. This condemnation, encouraged by some people for whom it served political purposes, weighed heavily on pastoral efforts in the years that followed, but it did not slow the trend it disapproved. In the seventeenth and eighteenth centuries, parts of the missal were published in many languages, especially for converts from Protestantism whose numbers increased in France once the Edict of Nantes is repealed in 1685.

The books that prove to be the most popular were very different in nature: these *Exercises for the Holy Mass* contained "considerations" or "uplifting reflections," ranging from allegorical meditations to paraphrases of the liturgical formulas. Their purpose was to enable the faithful to recite these formulas silently and thereby unite themselves with the priest. The authors of such works, for example, the Jesuits Nepveu and Gonnelieu, are ingenious at transposing without translating.

Christ's Sacrifice Is to Continue in His Members

It was Our Lord's desire that we receive in communion the sacrificial victim so that we take into ourselves the spirit and disposition of the victim, so that we become victims of God, so that we form all the church's faithful into one victim in Jesus Christ, something that one day will be perfectly accomplished in heaven. The Lord, one in himself, is nonetheless multiplied in these species in order to become a victim in many, making them a living victim, holy and pleasing to God . . . This, then, is Our Lord's intention as he multiplies his body and gives it in communion to the church: namely, to have as many bodies, as many mouths, as many hearts as there are subjects in the church; to offer himself in them for

>>>>>

the glory of the Father in as many places as there will ever be faithful in the world; thus to spread his love and his religion to all regions of the world; to extend this religion throughout the universe; and finally to have the whole world become one church, to have people everywhere share one religion, to have all voices utter one praise, to have all hearts become one victim. He is the universal and unique holy one of God his Father; he is extended into our hearts by the communion he gives us in his body.

J.J. Ouer, Ceremonies

"Explanations of the Mass"

Throughout the past five or six hundred years noted authors have written long treatises on the Mass. Those of Cardinal Lothaire, who became pope under the name of Innocent III, and of Durandus, bishop of Mende ... have been copied hundreds of times by subsequent authors who took from them whatever seemed more appropriate. But these authors, as skilled as they otherwise were, lacked experience in matters of antiquity and did not have time to do the necessary research ... Their genius was primarily exercised in the way they sought out and established would-be mystical interpretations throughout the whole Mass. These allegories, finding favor in the devotion of many people, were, nonetheless, never looked upon with universal approval. For a long time learned and educated people desired that the mysterious not be confused with the non-mysterious. In fact, as edifying as these interpretations might be for nourishing the piety of the faithful, they must take second place to what the early church believed. If necessity, convenience, or propriety gave rise to a ceremony one wishes to explain, then one must say so, and only afterwards go back as far as possible to discover the spiritual interpretation the church has, so to speak, added to the original reason for the ceremony. New interpretations should be considered last. The authors we have mentioned hardly follow this sequence; and it is for this reason that their works are less useful. We, in turn, are obliged to carry out the research they neglected.

P. Lebrun, Explication des prières et des cérémonies de la messe

This movement benefited, of course, from scholarly research on the ancient manuscripts. In particular, the monks of the Benedictine Congregation of Saint-Maur excelled in these studies: we have only to mention Jean Mabillon and Edmond Martène. Commentaries on the liturgy place the fruits of this historical research within reach of the clergy, offering thereby a basis for instruction among those whose degree of spirituality so allowed. An *Explication des cérémonies de la grand'messe paroissiale selon l'usage romain* appears, anonymously, in 1656, followed by similar treatises by the Benedictine Claude de Vert, the Sulpician Jean-Jacques Olier, and the Oratorian Pierre LeBrun, to mention only the most popular of these works.

Various Expressions of Eucharistic Devotion

The vast majority of Christians in the post-Tridentine era go to Mass only on Sunday, even when a parish mission is being held, and this schedule is significant. Even many priests do not celebrate every day. But

> **Priests Who Do Not Celebrate Every Day**
>
> I am here with three priest who act admirably. The one thing I lack in their company is the Mass.
>
> *Mme de Sevigne, Letter to Mme de Grignan, July 8, 1671*

an evolution in this practice became apparent in the eighteenth century. Daily celebration was incorporated as part of the royal court's schedule at the time of Louis XV and Louis XVI; it also appears in the regulations of all educational institutions, as something that can instill good ecclesial habits among the various levels of society. Thus, St. John Baptiste de la Salle makes provision for daily Mass in his treatise on the *Conduct of Christian Schools* which appears in 1720.

But the Mass is not the only demonstration of one's love for the eucharist. Devotions to the blessed sacrament and lengthy periods of adoration were also important in Christian life; churches belonging to the Jesuits held these practices in great esteem, and they were encouraged by the lay associations popular at this time. Since these devotional exercises fell outside the legal and regulatory concerns of rubricists, they allowed for the full expression of a piety that is elsewhere repressed. Polyphony, for example, held suspect by the Tridentine reform, creates in the popular realm a festive atmosphere, a place is made for the vernacular, and the exhortations given by the pastors establish a vital link between daily life and the presence of the Redeemer under the holy species.

Church buildings, whether characterized by the sobriety of the classical style or by the exuberance of the baroque, share a number of common traits that made them suitable for such devotional gatherings and for the celebration of the liturgy in its peculiar Counter-Reformation forms. Churches, resembling large festival halls, have galleries and boxes, and the way they are decorated calls everyone's attention to the imposing reredos (ornamental or wood screens) located on the wall of the apse. In all the churches a very large tabernacle predominates; above it rise pillars or columns separated by paintings or designs that greatly extol all the values rejected by the Reformers.

No longer is the altar the central focal point; its appearance is that of a long and narrow surface, hardly that of a table to be used for a meal. The Mass is celebrated at the altar by a priest wearing vestments that have become stiff and costly ornamental dress. His essential function is to bring about the real presence that the whole building honors. Above the tabernacle is a place constructed of gilded wood, on which the monstrance (or vessel) can be placed for "exposition" of the blessed sacrament, unless a central permanent niche has been reserved for this purpose.

With an undeniable pastoral design, everything was made ready for a court ceremony: just as at Versailles, Escorial, Potsdam, and the Schoenbrunn sumptuous feasts were prepared for the nobility and dignitaries of this world, so the most humble folks celebrate before the throne of the heavenly King, and their celebration leaves nothing to envy from celebrations glorifying earthly sovereigns. Here the faith and hope of all people are restored; here the faithful are renewed so that they may live according to God, despite the difficulties of daily life.

As popular as these celebrations were, they also revealed a lack of authentic liturgical piety. The most enlightened spirits, those whose aspirations were nourished by historical studies, continued to long for a more perfect realization of the projects inaugurated by the Council of Trent. Reform projects were initiated in Germany, especially by the bishop of Regensburg, Johann Michael Sailer (1751-1832), but it is in France that new missals appeared.

The "Neo-Gallican" Missals

For over a hundred years, from the second quarter of the eighteenth century to the middle of the nineteenth, a number of French dioceses used

110

their own books rather than the Missal of Pius V. These books are called "neo-gallican," but the term is inaccurate; they had nothing to do with the ancient Gallican tradition, and they faithfully followed the structure of the Roman Mass. A missal published in 1739 for Paris by Archbishop Charles de Vintimille quickly became the base document imitated by more than half the French bishops.

One feature of this reform is the greater number of formularies contained in the collection. These books had a greater selection of biblical readings; the number of prayers was increased by the addition of new texts drawn from ancient sacramentaries that research had recently rescued or composed according to the spirituality of the French School. A distinguishing characteristic of the sanctoral, the calendar of saints' days, was its attempt to reflect historical accuracy, and many chants were also revised to reflect the Scriptures more accurately. On the other hand, numerous sequences were introduced, notwithstanding that such a development did not harmonize well with the desire for a return to the sources.

Another characteristic of this movement was its tendency to search for themes inspired by the Gospel. Usually of a moralizing nature, these themes determined the general choice of texts.

The great richness found in the neo-gallican liturgy influenced future reforms. Yet it remained primarily the work of intellectuals, and rarely called for the assembly's participation. Still, it does not warrant the biased denunciations that resulted in its disappearance following a passionate struggle between its partisans and opponents in the middle of the nineteenth century.

* * * *

The Council of Trent renewed the way religious feeling and faith were expressed and made the Mass central to this renewal. In his *Introduction to the Devout Life* Francis de Sales speaks of the Mass as "the sun of the spiritual exercises," the "heart of devotion," and the "soul of piety." But this perspective is destined to harmonize badly with another product of Trent: the reformed missal. Participation by the faithful remains an ideal, something to be searched for. A great effort, based on extraordinary historical studies, was launched with the idea of explaining the rites of the eucharist, but the impression remains that this endeavor was not completely fruitful. Viewing the sacrifice as a means of expressing sorrow for sin and as a means for uniting oneself to the triune God through the death and resurrection of the Incarnate One surely has no connection with viewing the sacrament as the object of solemn and prolonged adorations.

A Bishop Introduces the New Missal to His Diocese

Bishops have always taken great care regarding the celebration of such a an august sacrament; they have carefully watched that nothing be introduced into the holy liturgy that could injure the majesty of such a great mystery; they have also called for the liturgy to be celebrated with dignity, in order to commend its benefits to the faithful and to engender in the hearts of the faithful a more authentic devotion.

Thus, in the spirit of the councils that have taken place over the past years, certain churches of Gaul have undertaken to reform and improve their missals (without, however, prejudice to the centuries-long practice of the whole Latin Church as to the regulation and ritual structure of the holy liturgy).

The needs that have been experienced required that this be done immediately . . . Assisted by some of the canons of our metropolitan church, we have decided to bring this project to completion . . .

We have chosen passages from Scripture that seem more apt for engendering piety, those that can be more easily sung, and those that best agree with the readings of the Mass. And yet our primary concern was that everything should serve . . . to elevate the spirit toward God and bring about the holy flame of faith, hope, and charity.

For the same reason we have added prefaces where proper prefaces were lacking, notably for the season of Advent and for certain solemnities celebrated during the year, for example, Corpus Christi, the Dedication, All Saints, and several others. In this way we have endeavored to enter into the ancient spirit of the Roman Church . . .

Nor has less attention been given to the orations said at each Mass . . . many of these are taken from the ancient sacramentaries, which are full of the unction of piety. As to new orations, the least possible number have been incorporated; insofar as possible these are modeled on the ancient

>>>>>

112

orations from which they often borrow a number of expressions . . .

We have borrowed these formularies from the most intelligible sources, especially from the sacramentaries of the Roman Church, mother and teacher of all others . . . It was, however, necessary to modify somewhat these prayers so as to shorten them, to eliminate obscurities, and to give them a more flowing style. This conforms to the tradition of all the churches which . . . when prayers pass from one liturgy to another, modify their wording while keeping the same meaning . . . .

We can affirm that we have religiously preserved the truths of Catholic dogma expressed by these formulas, and have done so without alteration or change.

L.C. de Choiseul, Missal of Albi (1763)

The connection is especially to be found in the sacrifice as the action necessary to effect the real presence of the blessed sacrament; but do people know that both sacrifice and sacrament concern one and the same act of worship?

Further Reading

Robert Cabié, *The Eucharist* 176-182.
Cheslyn Jones and others, eds., *The Study of Liturgy* 244-246.
Theodore Klauser, *A Short History of the Western Liturgy* 135-140.

Chapter IX

The Liturgical Movement and the Second Vatican Council
end of XIX - XX century

The popular practices described in the last chapter continued into the twentieth century, with even further decline of true liturgical participation, since the romanticism of the eighteenth century had encouraged the expression of deeply personal attitudes and promoted the spread of sentimental songs whose inspiration was far from biblical. On the other hand, the scientific work in progress had little impact on the formation of priests. To speak of liturgy at the beginning of the twentieth century was either to speak of minute and complicated rules governing the prayers and actions of priests and ministers, or to conjure an aesthetic and romantic feeling engendered by the pomp of external ceremonies.

During the second half of the twentieth century, however, a small group of priests and laity begin to discover other dimensions of the church's prayer, and as their reflection deepened, their numbers gradually increased. A new spirit that came to be called the "liturgical movement" was affecting their spirits and whetting their appetites for new forms of celebration inspired by tradition and responding to the aspirations of the most fervent among the Christian people. As a result, some limited reforms are permitted that help prepare the renewal that comes to fruition in the Second Vatican Council.

Liturgy, Source of Spiritual Life (1837-1909)

This course of events originated in the intuitions of a monk, Prosper Gueranger, who reestablished the Benedictine Order in France with the

Christmas Mass in an Abbey of the Congregation of Solesmes

The cantors leave their places and, standing in a circle in the middle of the choir, they sing the *Introit* as the abbot with his assistants begins the Mass.

At the *Kyrie eleison* the faithful come alive, and the young boys and girls from the village, led by their pastor, support the singing of the monks. The same is true at the *Credo* . . . Obviously, the singing here is not as flawless as at Solesmes, but this is another matter. What is projected is not art but the somewhat unpolished soul of a crowd that is moved for the moment; for a short time the primitive church is revived as the people, resounding in unison with their priests, truly participate in the ceremonies and pray with them by using the same musical language . . .

The Mass continues, with torrents of sound pouring forth from the organ. The abbot, wearing white socks and gloves, is sometimes at his throne, sometimes before the altar. His head is either bare or he wears a miter, made of linen and then replaced by one adorned with jewels. The abbot's hands are joined or he is holding his cross which he then gives to a kneeling novice who kisses his ring. Once the candles are lit, the smoke of incense hides the lancet arches, and the lamps by the relics shoot forth two flames of topaz into the blue clouds of smoke. Through the circles of perfume which ascend toward the arches, the motionless, gilded figure of the subdeacon can be seen at the bottom of the steps; at eye-level he holds the veiled paten till the end of the *Pater*. . . The Mass continues; the choir children, each with a lighted candle, kneel in a row during the elevation, which the sound of bells announces in the night; finally the *Agnus Dei*, with the abbot giving the kiss of peace from the altar to the deacon who descends the steps and in turn gives it to the subdeacon; the subdeacon, preceded by the master of ceremonies, extends the peace to the highest ranking cleric; he then gives it to the others who embrace and greet one another as they join hands . . .

The time for communion approaches; the ringing of hand-bells resounds in the apse; the novices and lay brothers, two

>>>>>

116

foundation of the abbey of Solesmes. Certainly we must distance ourselves from certain aspects of Gueranger's work. His spirit was thoroughly in line with the Counter Reformation, and he was inspired by an ultramontanism (a belief in papal supremacy) that nourished his fierce struggle against the French books which he accused of Protestantism and Gallicanism. He was, moreover, inspired by an admiration for the Middle Ages, and so misunderstood the true sources of liturgical renewal.

Nevertheless we are indebted to Gueranger for having created a community whose spiritual life was and is nourished by a lived experience of the church's prayer. Further, he carried this spirituality beyond the walls of his monastery by his various publications, especially the nine volumes of his *Liturgical Year* (1841-1866). Thanks to Gueranger, Christians again have a taste for the truth of the words, actions, and material things of the liturgy, the elements of celebration through which they share in the mystery of Christ. It is in this spirit that his successors at Solesmes undertook the work of restoring Gregorian Chant. Here was the beginning of a new way of gathering together for Mass.

The Reforms of Saint Pius X

It is in the liturgy, writes St. Pius X, that we find "the primary and indispensable source of the true Christian spirit." This, then, is the

117

direction that the faithful, encouraged by the this pope, begin to discover. The pope issued legislation on the church's chant and invited all members of God's people to receive communion frequently, even daily; in 1910 he allowed children who have attained the age of reason to approach the table of the Lord.

After rearranging the distribution of the psalms in the divine office, Pius X codified various additions and modifications in the Roman Missal; in 1914 he restored the Lord's Day to its true place—the number of saints' feasts had so increased that the Mass of the Sunday was only rarely celebrated. But to restore the full meaning of the liturgy—to see it once more as a participation in Christ's death and resurrection—the authentic character and central place of the Sunday assembly had also to be rediscovered.

To Follow the Mass (1909-1939)

The work of Lambert Beauduin, a Benedictine monk from the abbey of Mont César in Belgium, was the real impetus for the liturgical movement, which he also enriched by his interest in ecumenical matters. In 1909, he faced the future determined to bring the Mass to the people. To prepare priests for their task of education, he organized "Study Weeks" and began a periodical, *Questions liturgiques*. But the special medium for his activity was a small popular missal, published in the form of booklets; eventually this missal was replaced by Gaspar Lefebvre's *Paroissien* from the monastery of Saint-André in Bruges (the Saint Andrew Bible Missal), which was shortly to be found in the hands of all good church-going Christians. Not content any longer with a manual of prayers to be recited during the Mass, people now read the very liturgical texts, in Latin and in French. The drama at the altar was no longer hidden from them, but served to nourish their spiritual life. Similar efforts are undertaken for German-speaking Christians. Germany, of course, benefited from the theological research of Romano Guardini who in 1918 published his *Spirit of the Liturgy* and from Odo Casel, author of the *Memorial of the Lord* and of *The Mystery of Worship* in 1932. Also not to be forgotten was the popular impact of *The Year of Grace* by the Austrian Pius Parsch, a canon regular of Klosterneuburg. These reformers truly believed that a renewal of Christian life depended on the ability of ordinary Christians to participate in the church's prayers. This conviction and the resulting milieu led to the expression "pastoral liturgy": the joining of two words whose connection was not a familiar one at this time.

Perhaps somewhat awkwardly and yet inspired by the same spirit, the youth movement was also interested in the connection between liturgy and

118

The Whole Church Offers Sacrifice

[According to the Council of Trent] the Catholic priest offers the holy sacrifice in the name of and by virtue of the priestly power of Christ. And yet the priest is the representative of the whole church; it is the church which offers the sacrifice through the priest's ministry. The whole Christian people are consequently associated, to the extent determined by theology, to the role of the eternal priest, not only in principle and by right, but in fact and explicitly through the intermediary of the visible priestly ministry which Christ imparted to the hierarchy of the church.

Lambert Beauduin, Essai de manuel de liturgie

The Liturgical Movement and Catholic Action

During the years immediately following the war the liturgical movement became both widespread and reinforced. It became more popular and saw some immediate results. It benefitted from favorable circumstances, especially from the development of Catholic Action, in particular the Young Christian Workers movement. Father Cardijn was a friend of the abbey, and from the start of his apostolate he used to come for periods of recollection with his first members. When he began to organize large meetings, he entrusted the task of preparing the Mass to the abbey since the Mass was supposed to be the center of the day . . . To be sure, these meetings of young workers, with responses made to the priest, with singing the ordinary parts of the Mass, with participation in the offertory and communion, helped the liturgical movement gain more ground than many articles.

B. Botte, Le Mouvement liturgique: Témoignage et souvenirs

119

daily life; its members participated in "dialogue Masses" that used both the vernacular and the Latin.

The Assembly (1945-1962)

All that remains before there can be a full flowering of renewal is to recover the meaning of the assembly, a meaning that the vicissitudes of history had so forcefully obliterated. This recovery was made possible through the joint and providentially coordinated efforts of two groups: the priests and laity whose missionary spirit was aroused by the Catholic Action movement, so greatly encouraged by Pius XI; and liturgists whose historical studies had uncovered the fundamental dimensions of the tradition of the church.

The faithful are no longer content to "follow" the Mass by personally uniting themselves to what the "celebrant" does. The liturgical action requires a harmony of different actors, each having his or her own function and role which complements that of the other participants. The ministers and the entire assembly participate according to the place given to each by the sacraments they have received (baptism and ordination with its several degrees) and by the tasks to be accomplished in the celebration. The bishop or priest is once again the presider, not the person who does everything but one who acts in the name of Christ.

Moreover, the assembly assumes its full meaning only when Christ's disciples, called together and then dispersed for their task of evangelization, are sent forth into the whole world. Consequently, the missionary movement and the liturgical movement mutually nourish one another.

What Is Liturgy?

It is an error . . . and a mistake to think of the sacred liturgy as merely the outward or visible part of divine worship or as an ornamental ceremony. No less erroneous is the notion that it consists solely in a list of laws and prescriptions according to which the ecclesiastical hierarchy orders the sacred rites to be performed.

The sacred liturgy is . . . the public worship which our Redeemer as Head of the Church renders to the Father, as well as the worship which the community of the faithful renders to its Founder, and through him to the heavenly Father. It is, in short, the worship rendered by the mystical body of Christ in the entirety of its Head and members.

Pius XII, Mediator Dei, 25 and 20

After World War II this dynamism assumed an international dimension which further prepared hearts and spirits for the work of the council. Pius XII's 1947 encyclical *Mediator Dei* sanctioned the results of this work, thereby approving the desire of a growing number of Christians for a serious reform of the Mass.

The Last Reforms Before the Council

In fact, Pius XII established a commission, joined to the Congregation of Rites, to prepare necessary changes. The reform of the Easter Vigil in 1951 and of Holy Week in 1955, even if they do not directly affect the celebration of Mass, reveal a new way of understanding the relationship between priest and assembly, and thus look forward to the future. The council had not yet begun (though it had been announced) when these changes were collected and unified in the 1960 *Code of Rubrics*. This Code not only published the modifications that had already been enacted, it also added several further changes: the priest was to listen to the readings and no longer read them by himself when they were proclaimed by another minister; the *Confiteor* before the communion was eliminated; and the *Ite missa est* was replaced by another formula, e.g., the *Benedicamus Domino*, if the people were not dismissed, or omitted entirely if the liturgy continued. These directives were incorporated into the last typical (official) edition of the Missal of Pius V, which appeared in 1962. A final change was made the same year: St. Joseph's name was added after the name of the Mother of God in the eucharistic prayer. Such an addition is admittedly minor, but the eucharistic prayer had not been modified for centuries.

The Second Vatican Council

On 25 January 1959 Pope John announced his decision to convoke a council. An inquiry made of all the Catholic bishops in the world had indicated a pressing need for liturgical reform, especially in regard to the celebration of Mass. The most frequent requests concerned the use of the vernacular and concelebration. The draft of the Constitution on the Liturgy is drawn up by men accustomed to working together, accustomed to forging common convictions on fundamental points for a revision of the rites. The council, as early as its first session in October 1962, believed that this work was ready for discussion.

The final text of the constitution, the *Sacrosanctum Concilium*, was promulgated by Paul VI on 4 December 1963, after having received all but four affirmative votes. Its second chapter is devoted to the "mystery of the eucharist"; this chapter immediately follows the "general principles" that detail the nature and place of liturgy in the life of the church and the direction of the reforms proposed. The chapter begins by extending these principles as it recalls the sacrifice of Christ's body and blood, the memorial of the Passover, and the sacrament of love. In this light an outline of the reform is presented, thus sheltering it from any attempt to historicize or "archeologize" the liturgy and from innovations lacking any foundation in tradition. If the reform is far ranging; if, that is, it is necessary to look for a simplification of the rites, a suppression of doublets, and a restoration of elements that have disappeared (the general prayer), communion under both kinds, and concelebration (nos. 53, 55, 57-58), the intention is one thing: unity. The intention is to provide "a richer fare . . . for the faithful at the table of God's word" (no. 51) and to stress the unity between the liturgy of the word and the liturgy of the eucharist, since "they form but one single act of worship" (no. 56). The document's approach to the introduction of the vernacular is inspired by the same spirit (no. 54).

The Consilium for the Application of the Constitution on the Liturgy

Once the council's project had been precisely laid out with doctrinal, spiritual, and pastoral consistency, its concrete realization was entrusted to a commission called, by way of abbreviation, the *Consilium*. It would require no less than five years to produce the new missal, but some conciliar decisions were carried out immediately.

On 25 January 1964 the motu proprio *Sacram Liturgiam* requires priests to give a homily on Sundays and holy days of obligation. On 26 September of the same year, the instruction *Inter Oecumenici* introduces the vernacular for certain parts of the Mass celebrated with the people's participation. The instruction stresses the proper character of the liturgy of the word, recommends the adoption of the general intercessions and has the priest sing or say aloud the prayer over the gifts, the *Per ipsum*, and the prayer that follows the Our Father (which itself is to be prayed by the whole assembly). Finally, the instruction also restores the formula "The body of Christ - Amen" for the communion of the faithful and suppresses the last gospel.

Pope Paul VI also used his authority to introduce other changes, mainly concerning the eucharistic prayer. Although called for by the Constitution on the Liturgy, these changes actually respond to pastoral needs arising from the spirit of the document; for example, in 1967 the Canon can be said "so that it can be heard," and it can be translated into the vernacular for use

The Mystery of the Eucharist

At the Last Supper, on the night he was betrayed, our Savior instituted the eucharistic sacrifice of his Body and Blood. This he did in order to perpetuate the sacrifice of the Cross throughout the ages until he should come again, and so to entrust to his beloved Spouse, the Church, a memorial of his death and resurrection: a sacrament of love, a sign of unity, a bond of charity, a paschal banquet in which Christ is consumed, the mind is filled with grace, and a pledge of future glory is given to us.

The Church, therefore, earnestly desires that Christ's faithful, when present at this mystery of faith, should not be there as strangers or silent spectators. On the contrary, through a good understanding of the rites and prayers they should take part in the sacred action, conscious of what they are doing, with devotion and full collaboration. They should be instructed by God's word, and be nourished at the table of the Lord's Body. They should give thanks to God. Offering the immaculate victim, not only through the hands of the priest but also together with him, they should learn to offer themselves. Through Christ, the Mediator, they should be drawn day by day into ever more perfect union with God and each other, so that finally God may be all in all.

The rite of the Mass is to be revised in such a way that the intrinsic nature and purpose of its several parts, as well as the connection between them, may be more clearly manifested, and that devout and active participation by the faithful may be more easily achieved.

For this purpose the rites are to be simplified, due care being taken to preserve their substance. Parts which with the passage of time came to be duplicated, or were added with little advantage, are to be omitted. Other parts which suffered loss through accidents of history, are to be restored to the vigor they had in the days of the holy Fathers, as may seem useful or necessary.

Vatican Council II, Constitution on the Sacred Liturgy,
47-48, 50

A Journalist Describes a Session of the Council

Naturally the most solemn moment is the strictly religious ceremony that opens each session. On Wednesday morning it was a concelebrated Mass by the Melchite archbishop of Beirut, who was accompanied by two priests and a deacon. The majority of the bishops, unacquainted as they were with the majesty of the rite of "Antioch and Constantinople," were struck by the use of the Greek and Arabic languages, and were favorably surprised by the singing of the students from the Pontifical Greek College at Rome . . .

Most of the interventions focused on the use of Latin in the liturgy. The members of the Curia who spoke in its favor were in a minority, and their remarks were unsuccessful. Msgr. Bacci, for example, mentioned the expression "vinculum unitatis" (the bond of unity), and yet this adage is contested since the use of Latin has, in fact, created numerous divisions within the church. Cardinal Tisserant recalled that many languages have had--and still have—a legitimate place in the church, for example, Slavonic in the ninth century at the time of Cyril and Methodius. As one bishop from Madagascar put it, "the universal nature of the church does not depend on a language."

In a press conference to French journalists, Msgr. Jenny, auxiliary bishop of Cambrai and a member of the liturgical commission, made a point of insisting that unity in the church is to be reestablished around the altar and not around the clergy. He showed how the rites came to be weighed down during the Middle Ages, as well as the subsequent harm done to the liturgy by the abuse of the juridical spirit and by "rubricism," which were the consequences of the Counter-Reformation.

H. Fesquet, Le Monde, 31 October 1962

124

at Masses when the people participate. In 1968 the ancient Roman tradition of having only one anaphora is broken with the publication of three new formularies for the eucharistic prayer.

Eucharistic Concelebration

The Constitution on the Sacred Liturgy provides for the extension of concelebration "whereby the unity of the priesthood is appropriately manifested" (no. 57). The rite, promulgated in 1965, is so arranged as to make evident both the unity of the sacerdotal ministry and the unity of the Lord's sacrifice; for example, no private Mass is to be celebrated at the same hour in the same church.

The bishop is the true presider at concelebration, and the presbyterium surrounding the bishop only acts with him. We might say that the presidency is collective when the bishop is not present, since the principal celebrant is only a *primus inter pares*; any priest can fulfill this role; and, unless there are practical reasons to the contrary, he might be assigned for this at the last moment, as is done in some Eastern Churches. Nonetheless, it is important that this collegial ministry be represented by one person who greets the assembly, dialogues with it, says the presidential prayers (a few prayers are said by all), and blesses the assembled people. The other priests manifest their participation in the common action in ways determined by the church: for example, the words said by all that form the very heart of

> **Eucharistic Concelebration**
>
> Unless the needs of the faithful (which always must be regarded with a deep pastoral concern) rule it out, and without prejudice to the option of every priest to celebrate individually, this excellent way for priests to celebrate Mass is preferable in communities of priests, their periodic meetings, or in other similar circumstances. Those who live in community or serve the same church should gladly welcome visiting priests to concelebrate with them.
>
> *The Instruction Eucharisticum Mysterium of 1967, 47*

the eucharistic prayer, the intercessions which are distributed among several concelebrants, and certain gestures like the imposition of hands at the invocation of the Holy Spirit, and the extension of the right hand when the concelebrants say the words "This is my body ... the cup of my blood."

The action of the concelebrants takes place within the framework of the participation of all, and the circle they form around the altar remains open

125

on the side where the faithful are located. The unity expressed by this rite embraces the whole priestly people as its members surround those who have received the grace of presiding.

* * * *

Prepared for by the research and efforts of the liturgical movement, the conciliar Constitution on the Liturgy brings forth new forms of celebration. These forms both respond to contemporary needs, and they are deeply rooted in ancient tradition. They go beyond the earlier reforms in that they reach beyond the changes that occurred during the Middle Ages. The liturgy as carried out today presumes an inner renewal and a deep experience of ecclesial life. A number of the constitution's proposals were outmoded almost as soon as they appeared in light of the decisions made by Pope Paul VI to perfect its concrete application. But the essential vision remains: that the faithful be "able to express in their lives and manifest to others the mystery of Christ and the real nature of the true Church" (SC 2).

Further Reading

Bernard Botte, *From Silence to Participation: An Insider's View of Liturgical Renewal*, tr. John Sullivan (Washington, D.C.: The Pastoral Press, 1988).

J.L. Cunningham, "Liturgical Movement, Catholic," *New Catholic Encyclopedia*, vol. 17, 358-359.

Frederick R. McManus, "American Liturgical Pioneers," in *Catholics in America*, ed. Robert Trisco (Washington, D.C.: NCCB, 1976) 155-158.

Olivier Rousseau, *The Progress of the Liturgy: An Historical Sketch: From the Beginning of the Nineteenth Century to the Pontificate of Pius X* (Westminster, MD: The Newman Press, 1951).

Chapter X

The Missal of Paul VI
1969 - 1992

On 3 April 1969 Pope Paul VI signs the apostolic constitution promulgating the *Roman Missal Revised by Decree of the Second Vatican Council*. This decree, accompanied by an important *General Instruction*, introduces the new structure of the Mass. The missal, published in 1970, underwent a second typical edition in 1975. The new edition contains a number of minor revisions. In contrast to its Tridentine predecessor, this book does not include the scriptural readings. The typical edition of lectionary, also published in 1970, likewise appears in two successive forms. The books are translated into various languages. The English translation of the missal is published in 1972; that of the lectionary in 1971.

The Spirit of the Reform

The General Instruction on the Roman Missal (hereafter, GI) has a form completely different from the *General Rubrics* of the 1570 Missal. Replacing the general description of the rites is an introduction to the celebration; in this introduction doctrinal and pastoral considerations are primary and give meaning to the rubrical directives. This document, as the Latin *instruction* indicates, is motivated by a desire to teach. To the extent that rules are given, they are explained by referring to the most authentic and purified tradition and by linking them to the pastoral aspirations of the church, which is the "sacrament" of salvation brought by Jesus Christ.

The introduction to the general instruction affirms the continuity of Catholic doctrine. It speaks of "unchangeable faith" and "uninterrupted tradition," as it recalls the sacrificial nature of the Mass, the mystery of the

The Liturgical Reform:
Change of Rites or Change of Spirit?

According to information I received this past May from the Consilium charged with executing the liturgical reform, it is estimated that there are 205 languages in which certain sections of the Roman liturgy are now being celebrated. This past July I was in Canada where in the churches I visited I saw the altar facing the people, the ambo holding the lectionary, a chair for the celebrant, and, most often, a stand on which was placed the Latin-French missal. In the same country, thanks to the publication of weekly booklets for the faithful which contain the texts for the proper of the Mass, numerous are the assemblies that recite these texts in French, when they are not sung, leaving to the celebrant only the prayers belonging to the priest. A national Mass has been issued for the singing of the ordinary in French, and I heard this vigorously sung in various places.

All those who have traveled in France or in other countries can make similar observations: a number of changes have already taken place in liturgical life. These changes are especially evident in the modification of sanctuaries, in the use of the new books, in the use of the vernacular, in the intervention of various ministers throughout the celebration.

But every pastor who is solicitous as to the essential values of the Kingdom of God asks himself the following question: do these changes bring with them that renewal desired by the council? Is the source of Christian life, namely, God's word, the sacraments, and the worship of the church, truly more accessible to the faithful? Or have we merely replaced a traditional and familiar way of doing things with a different way of doing things, pleasing to some and displeasing to others, but in the end limited to the domain of ritual action and all the more to that of religious feeling?

. . . It must be said that the profound bond between liturgical celebration and one's life as a Christians appears, in many aspects, as difficult to obtain today as it was in the past. Let us frankly recognize that liturgical reform has not been completed; it has hardly begun.

Joseph Gelineau, La Maison-Dieu 84 (1965)

Lord's real presence under the forms of bread and wine, and the meaning of ministerial and baptismal priesthood. Using the words of Pius V, it evokes the "tradition of the Fathers" as presiding over a renewal for our time.

The spirit of the new missal is especially revealed by its constant and underlying preoccupation with the assembly as the first actor in the celebration. The normal or "typical" form of the Mass is a Mass at which the people are present. Adaptations to this norm are made according to particular circumstances; for example, Mass may be celebrated without a congregation. Such a celebration is certainly legitimate, though it only happens in exceptional cases. The liturgical books no longer concern only the priest and other ministers or clergy; no longer is there the same strictness about the number, status, culture, or concrete circumstances of the people once referred to as "those assisting." Many choices are now possible, and they are determined with the people in mind. The priest is constantly reminded to consider the spiritual good of the faithful more than his own preferences. He is even to consult with the laity about matters that more directly belong to them (GI 313).

The primordial status of the assembly does not stand in opposition to the functions of the various ministers; on the contrary, it requires these ministers so that the sign of Christ's mystical body can be fully constituted. The presider's task, whether bishop or priest, is to serve "God and the people with dignity and humility." He exercises this service by reason of his ordination through which "he presides over the assembly . . . through Christ" (GI 60). Other ministers are called as the needs of the assembly require. Three such ministers appear to be especially important because their presence constitutes the "typical form" of the Mass: the reader, who will usually be a layperson (GI 66); the cantor or psalmist to lead the sung participation of the assembly; and at least one minister of the altar. Other ministers are added "occasionally" or as the form of celebration or the number of participants requires (GI 65, 68, 69). This presentation is an understanding of ministries based on truth; priests will no longer vest as deacons or subdeacons, and mitered prelates will no longer be called on to "heighten the pomp of the ceremony." This reform is clearest in regard to the bishop's role as presider: "This is not done to add external solemnity, but to express in a clearer light the mystery of the Church, which is the sacrament of unity" (GI 59).

Introductory Rites

"After the people have assembled. . ." These words are among the first words found in the Order of Mass; they also appear in the General

Instruction (GI 25). The introductory rites facilitate the people's passage from a dispersed and scattered community in everyday life into a united and purposeful assembly.

1. The *entrance song* helps the faithful enter deeply into the spirit of the celebration; it should, therefore, provide for the people's active participation in a refrain or an "opening antiphon." The song should also lead them into the mystery of the liturgical season or feast. Moreover, because this

---

The Vernacular: A Pastoral Necessity

Among the first initiatives decided in implementing the Constitution on the Liturgy . . . was to give particular attention to the introduction of popular languages into the liturgy of the church, as pastors of souls and the faithful have desired for so many years.

At Mass the faithful "offering the immaculate victim, not only through the hands of the priest but together with him . . . should learn to offer themselves" (SC 48) . . . But this can only take place with the full and active participation of the whole people of God; pastors, then, will increase their efforts so that the people do what is entrusted to them; till the present the people have been silent and passive; now they are to become a living, attentive, and active people who participate internally in the mystery of salvation. This is to be the fruit of the liturgical life itself, and should penetrate to the innermost parts of the soul; it should, furthermore, promote this true and sincere dialogue, interior and spontaneous, between the faithful and God. . .

This understanding, if it is to be truly effective and not merely speculative and theoretical, must be be closely joined to the celebration of the liturgy—it must be experienced. And this requires the use of the vernacular together with a simplification of the rites. Every form of teaching or education is, in fact, communicated by words and actions, in a language understood by the eye and the heart. . .

The introduction of the vernacular into the liturgy is especially justified by the pastoral need to make celebrations understandable.

René Boudon, Bishop of Mende, Congress of Translators, 1-13 November 1965

song accompanies the entrance of the presider, it should begin and conclude with this action. The gospel book is normally carried by the deacon who then places it on the altar.

> After the people have assembled, the entrance song begins as the priest and the ministers come in. The purpose of this song is to open the celebration, intensify the unity of the gathered people, lead their thoughts to the mystery of the season or feast, and accompany the procession of priest and ministers. The entrance song is sung alternatively either by, the choir and the congregation or by the cantor and the congregation; or it is sung entirely by the congregation or by the choir alone.
>
> *General Instruction of the Roman Missal, no. 25-26*

2. The presider's *greeting* to the people and their response is restored to its appropriate place, namely, at the very beginning of the liturgical action. This dialogue indicates that the Lord, represented by the ordained minister, is present and that the gathering is spiritual in nature; it is not human initiative, but God who calls the people together. The presider may choose one of three texts: in addition to the traditional "The Lord be with you," or, for bishops, "Peace be with you," there are two others, both based on Scripture. The response "And also with you" alludes to the Spirit received through the sacramental imposition of hands; this response can be replaced after the second or B formula by "Blessed be God, the Father of our Lord Jesus Christ," an expression inspired by the Jewish "Blessed be God now and forevermore."

The sign of the cross precedes the greeting. If the people respond *Amen* to the signing, then the greeting no longer constitutes, as it did in antiquity, the first exchange between the presider and the assembly. To remedy this weakness, some episcopal conferences, like those of Germany and of French-speaking countries, have the priest alone say the *Amen*. The people do not speak therefore until they respond to the initial greeting, a decision approved by the Congregation for Divine Worship.

The greeting may be extended by a brief introduction to the liturgy of the day.

3. The *penitential rite* is an entirely new feature of this missal since, in the past, the *Confiteor* was the minister's private prayer in which the people did not participate, and since the *Kyrie*—which primarily expresses intercession—also has a clearly penitential meaning.

4. The *Glory to God* is now more clearly a festive element; it is sung or said only "on Sundays outside Advent and Lent, on solemnities and feasts, and in special, more solemn celebrations" (GI 31).

5. The *opening prayer* or *collect* is introduced by "Let us pray" and a period of silence. Its text, proper to each Mass, is the formula that offers the most variety; and in some cases this prayer is the only formula expressing the proper character of a particular Mass. The Collect always ends with the trinitarian conclusion followed by the assembly's *Amen*.

The Liturgy of the Word

The liturgy of the word is no longer the "fore-Mass," to use an expression that was sometimes employed in the past. It is not simply a preparation for the sacrament to follow. The liturgy of the word is an integral part of the celebration; it brings about the Lord's presence in the midst of the people since, according to the Constitution on the Sacred Liturgy, "it is he himself who speaks when the holy Scriptures are read in the Church" (SC 7), and the faithful are truly nourished at the "table of the word" (SC 51). Further, it is essential that "the intimate connection between words and rites may stand out clearly in the liturgy" (SC 35).

> Readings from Scripture and the chants between the readings form the main part of the liturgy of the word. The homily, profession of faith, and general intercessions or prayer of the faithful expand and complete this part of the Mass. In the readings, explained by the homily, God is speaking to his people, opening up to them the mystery of redemption and salvation, and nourishing their spirit; Christ is present to the faithful through his own word. Through the chants the people make God's word their own and through the profession of -faith they made their adherence to it. Finally, having been fed by the word, they make their petitions in the general intercessions for the needs of the church and for the salvation of the whole world.
>
> *General Instruction of the Roman Missal, no. 33*

1. On Sundays and solemnities two *scriptural readings* precede the gospel, only one at other celebrations. Their proclamation is entrusted to a reader. The gospel is proclaimed by a deacon or, in his absence, by a priest other than the presider; or if there is no other priest, the gospel is proclaimed by the presider himself. Its proclamation is surrounded with

solemnity and preceded by the traditional greeting and announcement. According to the missal, everyone present says after the readings the private formulas found in the Missal of Pius V; they are introduced by the words "The Word of . . ." In some places, these formulas are optional, except for the gospel: "Let us acclaim the Word of God—Praise to you, Lord Jesus."

The reading of the gospel still contains two private prayers: "Almighty God, cleanse my heart and my mind that I may worthily proclaim you" is said before the reading of the gospel (when a deacon proclaims the gospel, this prayer is replaced by a blessing from the presider), and after the reading the minister who has proclaimed it venerates the book with a kiss: "May the words of the gospel wipe away our sins."

2. The *chants*. A cantor or psalmist sings the *responsorial psalm* after the first reading, or it is given by a reader; the assembly participates by singing or saying a refrain; thus a dialogue is established between God and the people who respond using the very words of the Lord.

The *Alleluia* is sung before the gospel, usually during the procession from the altar to the ambo. It encloses a biblical verse. During Lent the *Alleluia* is omitted, replaced by a "gospel verse." This acclamation is intended to be sung; if it is not sung, it should be omitted. The sequences from the old missal (1570) are retained and placed before the *Alleluia*. They are always optional, except at Easter and Pentecost.

3. The *homily* is restores as an integral part of the liturgy of the word. It is normally given by the presider. It is based on the scriptural passages that have been proclaimed or on "another text from the Ordinary or from the Proper of the Mass" (GI 41). It is here that the mystery celebrated and the life of the faithful come together.

4. The *profession of faith* reminds us that we have been baptized, that we have received the word, that we can approach the sacrament. It shows that each person as a member of the community adheres to the church's rule of faith; the creed is said or sung on Sundays throughout the year, on solemnities, and on other days when its importance is to be stressed. It is replaced by the profession of baptismal promises at the Easter Vigil and at celebrations of baptism during Mass.

Structure of the Lectionary

1. On Sundays most pages of the four Gospels are read in the assembly: they are distributed over a three year period: Matthew in year A; Mark in year B; and Luke in year C. Since Mark's Gospel is shorter than the others, chapter 6 of John's Gospel, relating the multiplication of the loaves and the

133

The Old Testament and the Sunday Readings

The introduction of a reading from the Old Testament at all Sunday Masses (except during the Easter Season) is surely the greatest innovation of the Lectionary of Vatican II. As we know, the previous system of two readings never assigned an Old Testament reading to a Sunday . . .

The 171 pericopes of the Sunday lectionary are, to be sure, presented in a scattered fashion, since they are generally linked to the gospel for the day. And yet care was taken that these pericopes give a true insight into the entire Old Testament. What we have here is something like the pieces of a puzzle whose overall picture can eventually take shape in the minds of the faithful, provided there is suitable instruction. This implies that outside the celebration there be an initiation imparted by catechesis or by another means. With this as our preamble, let us examine the biblical table of the lectionary.

As a whole, the pericopes are short . . . This case for brevity corresponds rather well to the compact style of the prophetic writings; it excludes a good number of historical accounts or necessitates the omission of "essential" verses, all to the detriment of their living character . . .

Whoever wishes to highlight the Old Testament in the Sunday liturgy certainly cannot, with the texts as they are, look for a coherent linear path. And yet, on the one hand, it is possible to take special note of those rich texts whose particular merit calls us to pause for a moment to give them special attention . . . On the other hand, the lectionary permits a very rich reflection on the relationship existing between the two Testaments, not in a monolithic plan, but by presenting the diversity of living connections, of continuities, of tensions, even of contrasts which these two shutters of Scripture connect, thus better allowing us to appreciate the living reality.

Claude Wiener, La Maison Dieu 166 (1986) 47-60

discourse on the bread of life, is read from the seventeenth to the twenty-first Sundays in year B; however, it is especially during Lent and the Easter Season that the fourth Gospel is proclaimed. It serves as a type of sacramental catechesis and explains the mysteries of Easter and Pentecost. This semi-continuous reading allows the assembly to discover the richness of the "good news of Jesus Christ." The diversities, highlights, and various emphases of individual authors and the communities for whom they wrote bespeaks this richness.

The first reading is usually from the Old Testament. An attempt was made to select passages that correspond to the gospels: words or events recalled by Christ, or the progress made by people of the Bible toward the mystery yet to be revealed. In accord with ancient tradition, during the Easter season the Old Testament reading is replaced by the Acts of the Apostles.

The second reading is a selection taken from the Book of Revelation, the Letters of Peter and John during the Easter Season, and those of James and Paul during the rest of the year.

2. In Ordinary Time the gospel readings are arranged in a single cycle, repeated each year; the first reading, however, differs every two years. During the seasons of Advent, Christmas, Lent, and Easter, both readings are the same each year. The principle followed in selecting the readings was something of a compromise between choosing readings to fit the mysteries of the particular celebration and providing a semi-continuous reading, especially of the gospels.

3. Other schemata are followed for the feasts of the saints, ritual Masses, and Masses for various needs and occasions. For pastoral reasons a certain degree of freedom is permitted concerning the choice of readings.

General Intercessions

By means of the general intercessions "the people, exercise their priestly function to intercede for all humanity" (GI 45). After an absence of fourteen centuries, this prayer of intercession is now restored. Introduced by an invitation to pray and concluded by a collect (prayed by the presider), the intercessions are a litany led by a deacon or a member of the laity who calls to mind various human needs. Always, the whole assembly makes the intercession, either by means of a common invocation, expressed as a text of supplication, or by means of a silence after each intention. So that this prayer will be truly general, a fourfold schema is provided. The following headings indicate the general nature of the intentions: "for the needs of the Church; for public authorities and the

The Preparation of the Gifts

At the beginning of the liturgy of the eucharist the gits, which will become Christ's body and blood, are brought to the altar.

First the altar, the Lord's table, which is the center of the whole eucharistic liturgy, is prepared: the corporal, purificator, missal and chalice are placed on it (unless the chalice is prepared at a side table).

The gifts are then brought forward. It is desirable for the faithful to present the bread and wine, which are accepted by the priest or deacon at a convenient place. The gifts are placed on the altar to the accompaniment of the prescribed texts. Even though the faithful no longer, as in the past, bring the bread and wine for the liturgy from their homes, the rite of carrying up the gifts retains the same spiritual value and meaning.

This is also the time to receive money or other gifts for the church or the poor brought by the faithful or collected at the Mass. These are to be put in a suitable place but not on the altar . . .

The gifts on the altar and the altar itself may be incensed. This is a symbol of the Church's offering and prayer going up to God. Afterward the deacon or other minister may incense the priest and the people.

General Instruction of the Roman Missal, no. 49-51

salvation of the world; for those oppressed by any need; for the local community" (GI 46).

Preparation of the Gifts

The goal of the revised preparation of the gifts (formerly called the Offertory) is to avoid the ambiguities, introduced during the Middle Ages that led to various questionable interpretations. In times past, many Christians thought that they were to offer themselves at this moment, with their undertakings and labors, like a sacrifice before the sacrifice. But indeed the one sacrifice of Christ already involves the faithful in its own movement. To prevent this misunderstanding, the name given to this collection of rites has been changed. No longer is it the "offertory"; it is now called the "preparation of the gifts." Also removed are all the · unwarranted gestures and words of offering that appeared, as we have seen, to anticipate the eucharistic prayer. The essential action here is to bring forward the bread and the wine and to place them on the table, while the priest says, quietly or aloud, two "blessings": "Blessed are you, Lord, God of all creation. Through your goodness we have this bread (this wine) to offer . . ." Here, once more, are the simplicity and truth of the ancient Roman liturgy.

The request formerly made to the ministers directing them to pray for the priest is now an invitation for the whole people to proceed to the eucharistic action: "Pray, brethren, that our sacrifice . . ." The prayer over the gifts, sung or said aloud, concludes the rite.

Eucharistic Prayer

The Missal of Paul VI contains, in addition to the ancient Roman Canon, three other eucharistic prayers. The first of these new prayers (after the Canon) is Eucharistic Prayer II, an adaptation of the prayer found in the Apostolic Tradition. Eucharistic Prayer III is a new composition, and Eucharistic Prayer IV was inspired by the structure of the eastern anaphoras, for example, the beautiful anaphora of St. Basil.

The decision to have all four prayers use the same version of Christ's words at the Last Supper entailed several modifications in the ancient Canon (now Eucharistic Prayer I): first, the phrase "which will be given up for you," found in the Gospels, was added to "this is my body"; second, the Lord's command "Each time you do this . . ." was simplified and made to agree with the scriptural "Do this in memory of me." Also, the words "mystery of faith," which had been said over the chalice now introduce the assembly's acclamation before the anamnesis said by the presider; and

The New Eucharistic Prayers

The year 1966 saw an intensification of the faithful's desire to hear in their own language not only the preface and the *Sanctus* but the entire eucharistic prayer. And yet it soon became apparent that a mere translation of the Roman Canon would not suit all pastoral situations: the difficulty of certain passages . . . would discourage assemblies lacking biblical formation; the length of the text would exceed the attention span of children. Thus it was urgent to make available a plurality of formularies, some being inspired by the best witnesses of tradition, others being more specifically designed to express the thanksgiving and intercession of contemporary men and women. This proposal, carried out within the liturgical Consilium, was presented by Cardinal Lercaro to the Sovereign Pontiff, who agreed to it on 20 June. The Consilium was given the task of "composing or looking for" two or three eucharistic prayers, to be placed after the Roman Canon which itself would remain unchanged. Care was to be taken that the new prayers respect the proper genius of the Roman rite and harmonize with the totality of the Latin liturgy.

The work began in the autumn of 1966 and was completed the following spring. At the eighth full session of the Consilium (10-19 April 1967) it was possible to submit four formularies to the judgment of the Fathers:

— two ancient formularies: an adaptation of the anaphora of Hippolytus, and a Latin translation of the anaphora of St. Basil (which was simplified, especially its intercession);

— two new formularies: a prayer that could be used on any days since it had no fixed preface, and a prayer developing and expanding the theme of the economy of salvation, along the lines of the anaphoras of the Antiochene type.

The Fathers were highly receptive to the proposal and approved it on 14 April. Nonetheless, they were sympathetic to certain pastoral objections against the adoption of the anaphora of St. Basil in the West; this was not abandoned but merely postponed till a later time.

P. Jounel, La Maison-Dieu 94 (1968) 39-40

before the institution account, the new prayer calls on the Holy Spirit in regard to the consecration of the bread and wine.

Communion

The communion rite is truly the outcome and result of the whole celebration, and the summit of everyone's participation. The rites preparing for communion no longer overlap but form a series of well-regulated and unified elements.

1. The *Our Father* is said or sung by the whole assembly. The prayer that follows no longer mentions the saints whose names appeared in the previous version, but it concludes on an eschatological note: "as we wait in joyful hope for the coming of our Savior, Jesus Christ." The people respond using a doxology found in the *Didache*; this acclamation appears in certain manuscripts of Matthew's Gospel, and it is traditionally found after the Lord's Prayer in the Eastern Churches and in churches of the Reformation: "For the kingdom, the power and the glory are yours, now and forever."

2. The *rite of peace*. When pastorally opportune, the deacon—or, in his absence, the presider—invites each person to exchange a sign of love with one's neighbor; the form of this sign can be adapted to the sensibilities of different cultures or assemblies. It is preceded by a presidential prayer, which in the Tridentine Missal was a private prayer said by the presider in preparation for his communion; the first person singular is now replaced by the plural.

3. The *breaking of the bread* is restored to its original meaning. During the singing of the *Lamb of God* the priest breaks the bread that will be used for the communion of the faithful. This rite "is a sign that in sharing in the one bread of life which is Christ we who are many are made one body" (GI 56c). The rite must be related to the council's statement: "The more perfect form of participation in the Mass whereby the faithful, after the priest's communion, receive the Lord's Body from the same sacrifice, is warmly recommended" (SC 55).

4. At the *communion* the people no longer say the "Lord, I am not worthy" three times, but only once; and the priest adds a verse inspired by the Book of Revelation: "Happy are those who are called to his supper." The communion song follows. Its "function is to express outwardly the communicants' union of spirit by means of the unity of their voices, to give evidence of joy of heart, and to make the procession to receive Christ's body more fully an act of community" (GI 56i). As the bread of life is presented, each person expresses his or her personal faith by saying "Amen."

The council decided to restore, in certain circumstances, the laity's communion from the chalice. Although the reality is the same whether a person receives under one form or both, the sign of receiving under both best expresses the fullness of the sacrament's largesse. Conforming to biblical symbolism, the bread particularly recalls the assimilation of life, nourishment for the journey, and conviviality around the same table; the cup is a sign of festivity and holds the first fruits of the banquet in the Kingdom.

> ## Communion of the Faithful from the Chalice
>
> Holy communion has a more complete form as a sign when it is received under both kinds. For in this manner of reception (without prejudice to the principles laid down by the Council of Trent, that under each element Christ whole and entire and the true sacrament are received), a fuller light shines on the sign of the eucharistic banquet. Moreover, there is a clearer expression of that will by which the new and everlasting covenant is ratified in the blood of the Lord and of the relationship of the eucharistic banquet to the eschatological banquet in the Father's kingdom.
>
> *Instruction Eucharisticum Mysterium of 1967, no. 32*

In addition to the adaptations permitted by the missal, other changes may be made at the discretion of national episcopal conferences.

The ancient custom of receiving the eucharist in the hand can be restored, the choice, in fact, being left to the individual communicant; in no way is the minister to interfere with the communicant's freedom in this matter.

On the other hand, when there are not enough ordained ministers present, the church does not allow the faithful themselves to take up the bread or the cup. Instead the church calls on members of the laity to distribute communion; in this way the faithful will still receive the eucharist from another person and be able to respond *Amen* to a human voice witnessing that the bread and wine are indeed the Lord's body and blood. The reason for lay communion ministers is to show how important this personal dimension is to the church, and how this personal presence must be integrated into the totality of the sacramental action.

The communion rite concludes—after a period of silent prayer and, perhaps, a hymn of praise—with the prayer after communion.

Concluding Rite

Any announcements regarding the next assembly or the daily life of the community are normally made before the concluding rite, which is composed of the presider's greeting, a blessing that in certain circumstances can assume a more solemn form, and the dismissal given by the deacon. The rite is omitted entirely if another liturgical action follows immediately afterward, since the assembly would not, in that case, be dismissed.

Even though not called for by the rubrics, the assembly can leave the church singing, provided that this last song is not simply an excuse for detaining them.

Disputes in regard to the Missal of Paul VI

Shortly after the publication of the liturgy of the Mass in 1969, some Italian priests accused it of repudiating Catholic theology as formulated by the Council of Trent. They set forth their complaints in a pamphlet given to the pope by Cardinals Ottaviani and Bacci, who appended a letter requesting that the old missal might continue to be used. This letter was published in a number of Italian and French periodicals that were undertaking a campaign of vilification against the president and secretary of the Consilium, namely, Cardinal Lercaro and Msgr. Bugnini.

Cardinal Ottaviani complained that the letter was made public without his approval; he also said that he was satisfied with the doctrinal clarifications made by Paul VI in two discourses given in November 1969. The Congregation for the Doctrine of the Faith examined the dossier, and judged its accusations against the liturgy of the Mass to be without foundation. Nevertheless certain sections of the General Instruction were revised in order to avoid any further misinterpretations.

The debate did not end there. These attacks were a pretext for refusing the totality of the council's teaching: Marcel Lefebvre, a French missionary bishop and a member of the Spiritine Fathers, did not conceal his intentions in this regard, and gathered around him elements of resistance. To avoid aggravating matters, permission was granted to use the Tridentine Missal in certain cases but this tolerance did not end the schism. The pontifical commission "Pro Ecclesia Dei Adflicta," formed after the event, extended this permission, for the followers of Archbishop Lefebvre who did not follow him into schism; but the commission did not restrict itself to these cases or to only one missal. Unfortunately, these decisions are full of ambiguities and by no means serve true unity in the church today.

The Sacrifical Aspect of the Eucharist in the Missal of Paul VI

The Missal of Paul VI proposes the totality of the church's faith in regard to the Mass. The traditional doctrine is clearly presented in the apostolic constitution, in the introduction, and in the General Instruction, all of which are found at the beginning of the missal. These documents clearly affirm that the Mass is inseparably and at the same time a sacrifice continuing the sacrifice of the cross, the memorial of the Lord's death and resurrection, a sacred meal. All this should be kept in mind when giving catechesis so that one recognizes what it is that the church does, even if the church expresses this in various ways. For example, some express regret that the sacrificial aspect of the eucharist is not expressed in the new eucharistic prayers. But it seems that this aspect is stated there more clearly than in the Roman Canon. The summit of the eucharistic prayer is, in fact, the words of consecration when the priest emminently acts in the name of Christ. "In the words and actions of Christ, that sacrifice is celebrated which he himself instituted at the Last Supper, when, under the appearances of bread and wine, he offered his body and blood" (GI 55d). The words of Christ also express the sacrificial character of the celebration. His body is "handed over for you"—words which have been added in the new missal—and his blood "will be shed for you and for many."

The sacrificial character of the eucharist is furthermore expressed by the mention of the offering which is found in all the eucharistic prayers and by which "the church here and now assembled . . . offers the spotless victim to the Father in the Holy Spirit" (GI 55f).

Cardinal Knox, at the 1974 Synod of Bishops

Further Reading

Robert Cabié, *The Eucharist* 189-220.

Johannes H. Emminghaus, *The Eucharist: Essence, Form, Celebration* 101-212.

Frederick R. McManus, "The Genius of the Roman Rite Revisited," *Worship* 54:4 (July 1980) 360-378.

Lancelot Sheppard. "The New Ordo Missae," in *The New Liturgy*, ed. Lancelot Sheppard (London: Darton, Longmann & Todd, 1970) 19-40.

Conclusion

The Missal of Vatican II
A "Living" Book
1970 - 1992

Over twenty years have passed since the publication of the Missal of Paul VI. If on Sunday we enter various churches in the same city, at the time of the assembly, we will see the revised missal, as it were, on all altars. And no matter where we travel in the world, we will find it translated in all languages. Still, we are astonished by the variety of styles and how much the Mass differs from community to community. The rite of the Mass is the same everywhere, but it assumes many colorations. This variety, we dare say, is witness of the rite's fecundity: its primary objective, after all, is the "active participation of the faithful, both internal and external, taking into account their age, condition, way of life, and standard of religious culture" (SC 19).

It is, of course, possible to believe that the new liturgy could have responded even better to the reforms envisioned by the council. But no missal, of whatever kind, can totally express the celebration it makes possible: only in the concrete existence of Christian people does a missal come alive and bear fruit. The missal's success is in the diversity of the spiritual experiences it nourishes and transforms in the eucharistic action. In fact, as a result of the new rite a renewed manner of understanding the church, of living as church, has passed into our spirits and hearts. A certain way of establishing communication within the assembly, a world of sound no longer remote or foreign, the sight of laypersons reading the word of God, a way of addressing God and of extending one's hands to receive the sacrament of the Lord's body are so many elements that gradually fashion

145

a spirit of prayer and life in the church. We have not as yet received all the fruits of this human action that we share and whereby we enter into the mystery of Christ.

* * * *

During the past two decades the structure of the Mass has been officially enriched, and now new eucharistic prayers have been approved for use in certain churches. These do not have the same juridical value as the eucharistic prayers found in the typical edition of the missal (the Canon and eucharistic prayers II through IV) since they can be withdrawn from use or replaced. But, "As long as the Apostolic See has not determined otherwise," we can also use the three formularies for Masses with children and the two that were composed for the Year of Reconciliation (see the 15 December 1980 notification of the Congregation of the Sacraments and Divine Worship). Furthermore, in France the eucharistic prayer "For Large Gatherings" can also be used; this formula was approved for Swiss dioceses on the occasion of their synod (Decree of 2 February 1978).

Nonwestern countries are also making adaptations, as provided by the council. Thus, on 30 April 1988 the "Roman Missal for the Dioceses of Zaire" was promulgated. This missal borrows from indigenous customs: for example, the role of the "announcer" who presents the ministers and introduces the major parts of the liturgy, and the "invocation of the saints and upright ancestors" after the greeting by the presider. It also contains adaptations based on other liturgical traditions, for example, it places the rite of peace and even the penitential rite just before the general intercessions.

Finally, our journey down through the centuries has shown the reciprocal influences between eucharistic celebration and adoration of the blessed sacrament. This reciprocity was most noteworthy in the ritual promulgated in 1973: "The primary and original reason for reservation of the eucharist outside Mass is the administration of viaticum. The secondary reasons are the giving of communion and the adoration of our Lord Jesus Christ who is present in the sacrament. The reservation of the sacrament for the sick led to the praiseworthy practice of adoring this heavenly food in the churches."

Here the church acknowledges, although it insists first of all that the eucharist is food, and always remains food, that adoration of the sacrament is one of the great riches of western tradition. The tabernacle has no role to play during the Mass; the focus at Mass is on the altar, the ambo, and

146

the presider's chair. Nevertheless, the reserved sacrament should be kept in a place that favors meditation (GI 276), and permits liturgical prayer to be extended throughout the day and even the night by means of silent prayer.

Liturgical prayer, at least in its central part, is addressed to the Father through the mediation of the Son; but evangelical spirituality also elicits a desire to have dialogue with the Lord Jesus, to search for a deeper intimacy with him, to seek the humanity of the Savior in his proximity with us. In the East this legitimate desire has for a long time resulted in the veneration of the Icon of the Savior; in the West it gave rise to adoration of the blessed sacrament. As the ritual states: "Care will be taken that worship of the blessed sacrament appear in a relationship that unites it to the Mass"; thus it will be a thanksgiving for the gifts of God, a spiritual offering, intercession for the world, meditation on the mystery of Christ. It is an especially fruitful way of sharing in the attitude of Mary, the sister of Lazarus, who "sat at the feet of the Lord, hearing his words."

Acknowledgments

Chapter I

Scriptural selections from *The New American Bible with Revised New Testament*. Nashville: Thomas Nelson, 1987.

Pliny the Younger, Letter Written to Trajan. *Documents Illustrative of the History of the Church, Vol. I to A.D. 313*, ed. B.J. Kidd. New York: The Macmillan Company, 1938. (Revised.)

Justin, First Aplogy. *The Ante-Nicene Fathers*, vol. 1. Reprint: Grand Rapids: Wm. B. Eerdmans, 1989.

The Didache. *Ancient Christian Writers*, vol. 6. Westminster, MD: The Newman Press, 1948. (Revised.)

The Apostolic Tradition by St. Hippolytus. Lucien Deiss, *Springtime of the Liturgy*. Collegeville: The Liturgical Press, 1979.

Third Anaphora of St. Peter. Rev. Msgr. A. Detscher.

Eusebius of Caesaria, Church History. *Nicene and Post-Nicene Fathers of the Christian Church*, vol. 1. Reprint: Grand Rapids: Wm. B. Eerdmans, 1982.

Chapter II

Ambrose, On the Sacraments. *Saint Ambrose: Theological and Dogmatic Works*, tr. Roy J. Deferrari, *The Fathers of the Church*. Washington, D.C.: The Catholic University of America Press, 1963.

Egeria, Diary of a Pilgrim. Tr. George E. Gingras. *Ancient Christian Writers*, vol. 38. New York: Newman Press, 1970.

Augustine, Letter 54 to Januarius. Tr. Sr. Wilfrid Parsons, S.N.D. *The Fathers of the Church*. New York: Fathers of the Church, Inc., 1951.

Chapter III

Augustine, The City of God. *The Nicene and Post-Nicene Fathers*, vol. 2. Reprint: Grand Rapids: Wm B. Eerdmans, 1979.

Byzantine Anaphora of St. Basil. Louis Bouyer, *Eucharist: Theology and Spirituality of the Eucharistic Prayer*, tr. Charles Underhill Quinn. Notre Dame: University of Notre Dame Press, 1968.

Cyril of Jerusalem, Mystagogical Catechesis. Edward Yarnold, *The Awe Inspiring Rites of Initiation: Baptismal Homilies of the Fourth Century*. Slough, England: St. Paul Publications, 1971.

Chapter IV

The Prayer of Pope Gelasius. Joseph Jungmann, *The Mass of the Roman Rite: Its Origins and Development*, tr. Francis A Brunner; revised by Charles K. Riepe. New York: Benziger Brothers, 1959.

Gregory I, Roman Synod of 595. Robert F. Hayburn, *Papal Legislation on Sacred Music 95 A.D. to 1977 A.D.* Collegeville: The Liturgical Press, 1979.

Chapter VI

Thomas Aquinas, *Summa Theologica*, First Complete American Edition, literally translated by the Fathers of the English Dominican Provice, vol. 2. New York: Benziger Brothers, 1947.

Chapter VII

Council of Trent, Session 22. Robert Cabié, *The Eucharist*, vol. 2 of *The Church at Prayer: An Introduction to the Liturgy*, ed. Aimé Georges Martimort, tr. Matthew J. O'Connell. Collegeville: The Liturgical Press, 1986.

Martin Luther, The Babylonian Captivity of the Church. *Martin Luther's Basic Theological Writings*, ed. Timothy F. Lull. Minneapolis: Fortress Press, 1989.

Saint Andrew Bible Missal, prepared by a Missal Commission of St. Andrew's Abbey. New York: DDB Publishers, 1962.

Chapter VIII

Francis de Sales, *Introduction to the Devout Life*, tr. and ed. John K. Ryan. New York: Harper & Brothers, 1949.

Chapter IX

B. Botte, *From Silence to Participation: An Insider's View of Liturgical Renewal*, tr. John Sullivan, O.C.D. Washington, D.C.: The Pastoral Press, 1988.

Pius XII, Mediator Dei. James J. Megivern, *Worship & Liturgy*. Wilmington, NC: McGrath Publishing Co., 1978 (Translation © 1947, America Press).

Vatican II, Constitution on the Sacred Liturgy. *Vatican Council II: The Conciliar and Post Conciliar Documents*, ed. Austin Flannery. Northport, NY: Costello Publishing Company, 1975.

The Instruction Eucharisticum Mysterium of 1967. International Commission on English in the Liturgy, *Documents on the Liturgy 1963-1979: Conciliar, Papal, and Curial Texts.* Collegeville: The Liturgical Press, 1982.

Chapter X

General Instruction of the Roman Missal. International Commission on English in the Liturgy, *Documents on the Liturgy 1963-1979: Conciliar, Papal, and Curial Texts.* Collegeville: The Liturgical Press, 1982.
The Instruction Eucharisticum Mysterium of 1967. Ibid.